CRACKING *the* Oracle Apps DBA INTERVIEW

Stolen from Caminito

CRACKING *the* Oracle Apps DBA INTERVIEW

Joyjeet Banerjee

Principal Consultant
Oracle Consulting
USA

Tata McGraw-Hill Publishing Company Limited
NEW DELHI

McGraw-Hill Offices

New Delhi New York St Louis San Francisco Auckland Bogotá Caracas Kuala Lumpur Lisbon London Madrid Mexico City Milan Montreal San Juan Santiago Singapore Sydney Tokyo Toronto

Tata McGraw-Hill

Published by Tata McGraw-Hill Publishing Company Limited,
7 West Patel Nagar, New Delhi 110 008.

ISBN (13): 978-0-07-015282-3
ISBN (10): 0-07-015282-9

Managing Director: *Ajay Shukla*
Head—Professional and Healthcare: *Roystan La'Porte*
Publishing Manager—Professional: *R Chandra Sekhar*
Junior Sponsoring Editor—Computing: *Ritesh Ranjan*
Asst. Manager—Production: *Sohan Gaur*
Manager—Sales & Marketing: *S Girish*
Product Manager—Science, Technology & Computing: *Rekha Dhyani*
Controller—Production: *Rajender P Ghansela*
Asst. General Manager—Production: *B L Dogra*

Typeset at Bukprint India, B-180A, Guru Nanak Pura, Laxmi Nagar, Delhi 110 092

Cover Design: Kapil Gupta, New Delhi

RALCRDLFRXZYD

The McGraw·Hill Companies

To

my father

who left for heavenly abode when the book was in progress;

my mother, my sisters Joyeeta and Tiya,

my brother-in-law Sagar,

and

my sweetest niece Saanjh

Preface

This book is the result of meeting that I had with Deepa, formerly with McGraw-Hill. We were discussing about my book *Oracle Applications DBA* when Deepa asked me to include questions and answers at the end of each chapter to test the readers' knowledge on the domain and help them in preparing for Apps DBA interview. Further she suggested to develop a book covering all the frequently asked questions in an Apps DBA interview. I thought that the idea was great and I started writing this book.

Cracking the Oracle Apps DBA Interview covers most of the questions that are asked in a typical Apps DBA interview. By reading this book readers would be able to prepare for the Apps DBA interview. Here is the brief of what this book contains.

Chapter 1 focuses on Oracle Applications Architecture. It covers questions on architecture, file system, important configuration files, technological stack details, the various Oracle Applications components, etc.

Chapter 2 covers Oracle Applications Installation. It covers questions on both single and multi-node installations.

Chapter 3 discusses forms server. It covers questions on how forms server works, various components of forms server, configuration files, different modes of forms server, etc.

Chapter 4 focuses on concurrent manager. It covers questions on different kind of managers, how to enable PCP, GSM, work shifts, scheduling requests, start, stop, and define managers.

Chapter 5 is on patching. It covers questions on the entire patching flow, how to apply patches in interactive and non-interactive mode, how to apply multiple patches together, different modes of adpatch, patch failures, patch drivers, how to restart patching, patch tables, rolling back after patching, etc.

Chapter 6 covers all Ad Utilities.

Chapter 7 focuses on cloning. It covers question on cloning from single node to multi-node, multi-node to single node, adclone, rapidclone, autoconfig reducing time for cloning, etc.

Chapter 8 focuses on upgrading of Oracle Applications covering steps on upgradation, pre- and post-upgrade steps, etc.

Chapter 9 is on Release 12. It covers questions on the new features of Release 12 including R12 architecture, file system, unified APPL_TOP, shared file system, etc.

I would like to share a few tips that will help you clear any interview.

- **The first prerequisite for clearing a technical interview is knowledge:** Try to be a master of the subject and gather as much technical information as possible. If you are a subject matter expert, then no one can stop you from getting the offer letter.
- **Prepare well and work hard:** There are no shortcuts to success, so put as much effort as you can. Discuss the subject with your friends, colleagues and resolve all your doubts.
- **Know something about the organization:** Apart from knowing the subject, gather as much information as possible about the organization where you are appearing for the interview. Visit their website to find out about their products, turnover, etc.
- **Be confident and dress well:** Dressing well boosts your confidence and leaves a good impression on the interviewer. Though people sometimes wonder why dressing up is important for a technical interview. But from a company's point of view, all-rounders are preferred who are technically good as well as smart, confident, and presentable.

- **Stay calm:** During the interview don't get excited or start debating with the interviewer. Even if you think that the interviewer is wrong, don't try to prove that he is wrong. Follow the principle 'the interviewer is always right' to clear the interview, which is your goal.
- **Speak the truth:** If you don't know something simply accept it. Don't try to give a wrong answer or fool the interviewer. Your chances of clearing an interview are more if you accept that you don't know certain things rather than telling lies or bluffing. The interviewer also understands that no one has all the answers.
- **Listen carefully to the questions:** If you have any difficulty in understanding any question, then don't hesitate to ask the interviewer to repeat it.
- **Be clear about your present job responsibilities:** Quite a few interviews start with this question. Make sure you know all that you have written in your résumé.
- **Know your strengths and emphasize on your strengths while answering:** If you emphasize something, the next question of the interview is generally the point which you are stressing more. Try to stress more on your strong points to take the interview in the direction where you want it to take.

Comments, suggestions and feedback are most welcome and would be definitely acknowledged. You can mail me all your comments and suggestions at joyjeet.books@gmail.com. If you are stuck in any tricky question and unable to find a solution, feel free to write to me. I will respond to your email and will include them in the next edition.

JOYJEET BANERJEE

Acknowledgements

I am really thankful to all my friends who motivated me, as it would have been impossible to complete the book without their efforts. I would like to thank all my friends and colleagues especially Jaikant, Ravi, Hemant, Rajesh, Raja, Rajrupa, Subhodeep, Kumkum, Nirmalya, Saugata, Tanmoy, Sreelatha, Jyoti, Sugeeti, Sushma, Surbhi, Neha, Manjusha, Aparajita, Sharath, Aditya, Saurabh, Sunil, Sahil, Jyoti, Nagarjuna, Abhijat, Syed, Sanjeev, Nurul, Abhilash, Brajesh, Abhishek, Vikram, Divya, Vineet Bhatia, Susmita, Vineet Fernandes, Nikhil, Kapil, Anuj, Neeraj, Vinay, Sudhanshu, Suresh, Thiagu, Channesh, Santhosh, Jayaraman, Murali, and Sandeep for extending their help every time to make this book a reality.

I would also like to thank my manager Sanjay Bheemasena Rao and Kevin Dahmas for reviewing the book and helping me in getting all the approvals. I thank my manager Daniel Gonzalez and Dennis Horton for all the motivation. I would also like to thank Sreeni Hosamane and Shanna Gazley for helping me in getting all the approvals from Oracle legal department. I would also like to thank Rick Jewell for approving the book, and would like to thank Todd Alder and T J Angioletti for giving all the relevant approvals from the legal department.

This book would not have been possible without the help of the editorial and production teams at McGraw-Hill Education, India.

Joyjeet Banerjee

Contents

Preface *vii*

Acknowledgements *xi*

1. Architecture **1**
2. Installation **24**
3. Forms **36**
4. Concurrent Manager **42**
5. Patching **61**
6. Ad Utilities **76**
7. Cloning **90**
8. Upgradation **101**
9. R12 **112**

Index **131**

1
Architecture

1. Describe the architecture of Oracle Applications.

Oracle Applications follow a three-tier architecture: (1) database tier containing the RDBMS database, (2) middle-tier containing various servers like forms server, Web server, concurrent processing server, admin server, reports server and discoverer server, and (3) desktop tier, the client desktop, through which users access Oracle Applications.

2. Does a tier mean a physical machine?

No, a tier does not mean a physical machine. It is basically a logical portioning. Each tier has more than one physical server and each physical server can accommodate more than one different tier. For example, the middle-tier can be configured in 4-5 different servers and any server can be used for hosting database as well as Web server.

3. How is the three-tier architecture different from client server architecture model and which is a better model?

In a client-server architecture, you need to install the application software in all the client's machines. If you are using 100 computers as clients, you need to install the application software in 100 computers. The three-tier architecture eliminates this issue. The application software is hosted centrally in the middle tier and there is no need to install it in all the client's machines.

4. If I am not installing the client software in the desktop PC, then how will I access Oracle Applications?

The client desktop accesses Oracle Applications through Java-enabled Web browser with JInitiator and forms client applet.

5. What is forms client applet?

For running forms from the client computer, the forms client applet must run in the client desktop. It supports all Oracle Application forms including the custom forms. The forms client applet is a collection of JAR (Java Archive) files. These JAR files contain all the classes, required to run the presentation layer of Oracle Applications.

6. What is JInitiator?

Oracle JInitiator enables end-users to run Oracle forms services applications directly within Netscape Navigator or Internet Explorer on Windows 2000, Windows NT4.0, and Windows XP platforms.

Oracle JInitiator is implemented as a plug-in (Netscape Navigator) or ActiveX Object (Microsoft Internet Explorer). It allows you to specify the use of the Oracle-certified Java Virtual Machine (JVM) on Web clients instead of relying on the default JVM provided by the browser.

Oracle JInitiator is automatically downloaded to a client machine from the application server for the first time. The client Web browser encounters an HTML file that specifies the use of Oracle JInitiator. The installation and updating of Oracle JInitiator is performed using standard plug-in mechanism provided by the browser.

7. **Do I need to download and install JInitiator every time I log in to Oracle Applications?**

No, the JInitiator needs to be installed only once. After the JInitiator is installed, the client's desktop is configured and nothing needs to be done from the client's machine.

8. **What is Oracle Applications technology layer?**

Oracle Applications technology layer provides common basic functionality across all Oracle Applications product families. The Oracle Applications technology layer is a collection of products whose functionality is used by all the modules of Oracle Applications.

9. **What are the components of Oracle Applications technology layer?**

Oracle Applications technology layer comprises the following products:

- Oracle Application DBA (AD)
- Oracle Application Object Library (FND)
- Oracle Common Modules (AK)
- Oracle Application Utilities (AU)
- Oracle Alert (ALR)
- Oracle Workflow (WF)
- Oracle Applications Framework (FWK)
- Oracle XML Publisher (XML)

10. **What does database tier consist of?**

Database tier consists of Oracle database, which stores all the data. The database server contains Oracle Home and data files.

11. **How many Oracle Homes are there in Oracle Applications and what is the importance of each one of them?**

Oracle Applications have three Oracle Homes:

1. Database Oracle Home in the database tier that acts as the Oracle Home for the Oracle database.
2. Oracle Home in the application tier, also known as 8.0.6 Oracle Home. It is called the technology stack Oracle Home and used by forms, reports and discoverer.
3. iAS Oracle Home, used by the Oracle HTTP server. It is used by the Web listener.

12. Can I enable real application clusters in the database tier along with Oracle Applications?

Yes, real application clusters can also be configured with Oracle Applications. In that case, more than one instance of Oracle runs and the data files are stored at a central location accessible from the entire instance.

13. What does the application tier consist of?

The application tier is the place where the application software is located. It also hosts a large number of servers which interact with the database and the client tier. The application tier architecture shifts software administration from the desktop to the middle tier removing the burden of installing the application software at every client. The application tier also supports load balancing among multiple forms server, concurrent processing server to provide optimum scalability and performance.

14. Which servers are hosted from the application tier?

The following six servers constitute the application tier:

- Oracle HTTP server (Apache)
- Forms server
- Reports server

- Admin server
- Concurrent processing server
- Discoverer server

15. What is Oracle HTTP server?

Oracle HTTP server is the Web server which is used by Oracle Applications. It processes all the requests received from the clients. The Web server includes a couple of additional components like Web listener, Jserv (Java Servlet Engine) and Java Server Pages.

16. What is the difference between Apache and Oracle HTTP server?

Oracle HTTP server is the customized form of the Apache. Oracle has customized the Apache Web server as per its own requirement which is known as the Oracle HTTP server.

17. What is the function of the Oracle HTTP (Apache) server?

The Web listener accepts the HTTP requests coming from the client browsers, and the Web server services the request. If the URL needs advanced processing then it forwards the same to the servlet engine which in turn contacts the database for processing the request and returns back to Web listener. If the incoming request needs parsing a JSP file then the following sequence occurs. The client browser makes a request to the Web listener. The Web listener checks the nature of the request and then contacts the Jserv (Servlet Engine) where it runs a JSP. The JSP contacts the database for the information and returns a HTML page which is in turn displayed in the Web browser.

18. How does Oracle HTTP (Apache) server work?

The Web server works in the following way:

- The user clicks a hyperlink on his desktop.
- The browser contacts the Web listener with the URL. If possible, the HTTP listener services the request itself by returning a simple HTML page. In case it needs a JSP parsing then
  - the Web listener redirects the same to Servlet Engine (Jserv) for running a JSP;
  - the JSP in turn contacts the metadata dictionary in the database where it gets the information from the application tables to construct the HTML page;
  - the Web server returns the resulting HTML page back to the browser.

19. Where are Apache log files located, and what are these files?

Apache log files are stored in $IAS_ORACLE_HOME/Apache/Apache/logs. The log files are error_log, error_log_pls, access_log and access_log_pls.

20. Where are Apache configuration files stored and what are the important Apache configuration files?

Apache configuration files are stored in $IAS_ORACLE_HOME/Apache/Apache/conf directory. The main configuration files are httpd.conf, apps.conf, httpd_pls.conf, oprocmgr.conf, and oracle_apache.conf.

21. How do I know which file—httpd.conf or httpds.conf — is being used by the Apache?

The same can be determined by examining the script apachectl which is located at $IAS_TOP/Apache/Apache/bin. It is internally called by the script adapcctl.sh which is located at the scripts location. In the script apachectl, there is a variable httpd defined, which points to either the httpd or the httpds executable. If the httpd variable in the apachectl script calls httpd, Apache configuration depends on httpd.conf. If the apachectl script calls httpds, Apache configuration depends on httpds.conf.

22. In case of a shared APPL_TOP, where do I see the configuration files and the log files for the Apache?

In case of a shared APPL_TOP, the techstack home is also shared across all the different server so all the Apache and Jserv configuration files are stored in $IAS_CONFIG_HOME directory. There will be a separate $IAS_CONFIG_HOME directory for each node of the application system.

23. I have done a couple of customizations in apps.conf, jserv.properties but each time I run the autoconfig it is overwriting the customizations. What do I do?

To overcome this problem, go to the $FND_TOP/admin/template directory. There also, you will see all those configuration files. Make a directory custom in the $FND_TOP/admin/template directory and copy all the files where you want to do the customization from $FND_TOP/admin/template to $FND_TOP/admin/template/custom and do the customizations in the files in custom directory. Now run autoconfig. To explain this, lets take an example. Say you want to do some customization in the apps.conf file. The usual location of the apps.conf file is $IAS_ORACLE_HOME/Apache/Apache/conf. The same file is also available in the $FND_TOP/admin/template directory. Copy the apps.conf file from $FND_TOP/admin/template directory to custom directory. Make all the customizations in the apps.conf file in the custom directory. Now run autoconfig. The customizations will now be read from the files in custom directory.

24. Where are Jserv configuration files stored?

Jserv configuration files are stored in $IAS_ORACLE_HOME/Apache/Jserv/etc.

25. What are the important configuration files which are used for making Apache run along with Jserv?

- $APACHE_TOP/Apache/conf/httpd.conf (or httpds.conf, depending on your platform)
- $APACHE_TOP/Jserv/etc/jserv.conf
- $APACHE_TOP/Jserv/etc/jserv.properties
- $APACHE_TOP/Jserv/etc/zone.properties
- $APACHE_TOP/Apache/conf/oracle_apache.conf
- $APACHE_TOP/Ojsp/conf/ojsp.conf

Whereas $APACHE_TOP refers to the $IAS_ORACLE_HOME/Apache directory.

26. Where are Jserv log files located?

The Jserv log files are located in the $IAS_ORACLE_HOME/Apache/Jserv/log directory and in the format mod_jserv.log.

27. Where are JVM log files located?

The JVM log files are located in the $IAS_ORACLE_HOME/Apache/Jserv/log/jvm directory.

28. How do I check the version of Apache?

The version of the same can be checked using the command $IAS_ORACLE_HOME/Apache/Apache/bin/httpd –v. The output is given similar to as given below.

httpd -v

Server version: Oracle HTTP Server Powered by Apache/1.3.19 (Unix)

Server built: Dec 6 2005 13:41:10 (iAS 1.0.2.2.2 rollup 5)

29. When I login to the Oracle Applications from the PHP-based applications, login page simply hangs. What approach should I follow for the debugging?

If the login page hangs, the first step would be to check the Apache log files. Go to the Apache log directory and check for the access_log and error_log. You will get some information there. If you are not able to find anything then check for the Jserv logs from there you will get some information. Also, check the logs of the JVM. Try to analyze all the errors that you are getting from log files and try to fix them. Still if you are not able to debug anything then do an AOL diagnostics test which will tell you where the issue is. You can also enable debug for Apache, Jserv if you are not getting any pointer from the logs.

30. How do I enable debug for Apache?

Edit the httpd.conf/httpds.conf file to enable debug for apache. Find the following section in the apache configuration file and set the LogLevel to *debug*. You may want to make a backup of this file before you edit. Now the Apache log files will be written with the debug information. You also need to bounce the Apache after the making the changes.

31. How do I enable debug for Jserv?

Edit the jserv.conf to enable debug for the Jserv module. Find the following section in jserv.conf and set the LogLevel to *debug*. Also, edit the jserv.properties to enable debug for the java portion of the Apache jserv find the following section in jserv.properties and *set log=true*, *log.timestamp=true*, and the logging for the channels to true *log.channel=true*. You also need to bounce the apache after making the changes. Now the log files will be written with the debug information.

32. How can I launch AOL diagnostics test?

The AOL diagnostics test can be launched using the following URL.

http(s)://<host><domain>:<port>/OA_HTML/jsp/fnd/aoljtest.jsp

It prompts for the database hostname, SID, port name, apps userid and apps password. In case of RAC environments, you have to give the JDBC URL.

33. How do I know about the location of JDBC URL?

The JDBC URL is there in the DBC file in the $FND_TOP/secure directory. Open the file and you will get the JDBC URL from there.

34. How do I test whether my DBC file is valid or not?

You can check the validity of the DBC file using the *AdminAppServer* utility. Run the following command java oracle.apps.fnd.security.AdminAppServer appsun/appspw STATUS DBC=[path to dbc]/[dbc_name].dbc

This should return STATUS: VALID

35. I have accidentally deleted DBC file or my status of the DBC file is invalid, how do I recreate the same?

Run Autoconfig. It will recreate the DBC file else you can also create the same by running the script adgendbc.sh located at $COMMON_TOP/admin/install directory.

36. What is plsql cache and what is its importance?

The mod_pls component of the Apache caches some database content to file. The plsql cache also known as database cache is of the type session and plsql cache. The session cache is used to store the session information and the plsql cache is used to store the plsql cache which is used by mod_pls. It is stored in the $IAS_ORACLE_HOME/Apache/modplsql/cache directory.

37. How do I enable PL/SQL logging?

Edit the file wdbsvr.app, which is usually found in $ORACLE_HOME/Apache/modplsql/cfg/ and set the following two parameters—*debugModules=all* and *LoggingLevel=Debug*

38. What is admin server?

The admin server is that node of the APPL_TOP from which all the maintenance activities for Oracle Applications are performed.

39. What kind of maintenance activities can be performed from admin server?

The following maintenance activities can be performed from the admin server.

- Applying the patches
- Maintaining Oracle Applications
- Applying the ad utilities
- Upgrading Oracle Applications

40. Does admin server also have a process like Apache and forms server?

No, the admin server doesn't have an operating system process like Apache or forms server. It is basically a node of the APPL_TOP.

41. What is concurrent processing server?

When an Oracle Application user submits a request to run a program, it's called concurrent requests. Concurrent manager are the programs responsible for running the concurrent requests. Concurrent requests are processed from concurrent processing server.

42. What is forms server?

The forms server is that server from which the forms are hosted. It's a component of middle tier. The forms server can be hosted from more than one node and the load balancing can be implemented with the forms. The forms user interface is used in the desktop clients for working in Oracle Applications.

43. Explain briefly, how the connection of the forms server works?

This is how the forms server works.

- Browser sends request (URL) to HTTP Listener (Apache)
- HTML page is retrieved (static) or generated (dynamic)

When the Web server receives the URL, it interprets it. If the URL points to a static file, the file will be retrieved from storage. If the URL points to a CGI script, the file will essentially be the same as the static version, but some pieces of that file will be dynamically generated by the CGI script. If dynamic, CGI script asks load balancing server for least loaded server. If the URL points to a CGI script, the CGI script will poll the load balancing server.

The CGI script asks the load balancing server for the least loaded forms server. The load balancing server returns the answer, and that answer is used in the generation of the HTML file returned to the browser.

- HTTP Listener sends HTML page back to browser

Browser decodes HTML page, and detects the <APPLET> tag, indicating a Java Applet.

As the browser decodes the HTML file returned by the Web server, it detects the <APPLET> tag. This is the designator that indicates a Java Applet. Specifically, this is the thin client that will connect to the forms server.

The <APPLET> tag contains the name Applet, along with numerous parameters including (a) the name of the form to run, (b) the name of the forms server to use, (c) login information, and (d) any other parameters you need to pass to your forms session.

- Browser sends request (URL) to HTTP Listener for Java Applet

The browser asks the Web server to send it to the Java Applet. Java Applets are stored in .class or Java Archive (JAR) files. Oracle Applications use JAR files. JAR files are compressed archives that contain multiple .class files. Oracle Applications use JAR files because they speed up the downloading of the Java Applet. There are many JAR files that Applications must download to run.

- HTTP Listener returns Applet (JAR files) to browser

Browser receives Java Applet (JAR files) and begins to run them in its JVM (JInitiator). The JVM JInitiator checks the version of the files being sent. If the version of the JAR files is newer than the version cached on the client, JInitiator will continue the download. If the version is the same or older, JInitiator will begin to run the cached Java files. Java Applet is now running in the JVM. Browser is no longer part of the equation. The Java thin client connects to the forms listener via a TCP/IP socket or an HTTP port. The forms listener is already started, and listens for these requests.

- Forms Listener allocates a forms runtime engine

When the Forms Listener gets the request, it starts a new forms runtime engine for this thin client. This started forms runtime engine can either be a newly spawned process, or it can be an allocation of an already running process (which greatly speeds up the connection process).

- Java Applet connection is passed from Forms Listener to forms runtime engine

The Forms Listener hands-off the connection to the thin client, and then has no further role in the process. Forms runtime engine loads module(s) needed to run the requested form. When the thin client connected, it passed a parameter entry, serverArgs. In that parameter entry, there was a name of a form to run. At this point, the forms runtime engine loads the form and any libraries and/or menus required by that form.

- Forms runtime engine opens a connection to the database

The details of this connection depend on whether the Forms Runtime Engine is a newly spawned process, or if it was allocated from a pool of already running processes.

44. What is load balancing?

Load balancing is a server process that monitors loading on all of the forms servers. Each of the forms servers runs a load balancing client which keeps the load balancing server apprised of its load.

45. How can you find how many forms users are connected to the application system from the operating system level?

You can do the same by querying the f60webmx process and counting the same.You can use the following command to check this.

ps -ef | grep f60webmx | wc –l

46. In my PC, I can see lots of JInitiators are installed. How can I find which JInitiator is being used by the forms process?

When the forms is launched, the Java console displays all the information about the forms process. There it displays which version of the JInitiator the forms is using. Alrernatively, you can also open the appsweb.cfg file and check the parameter jinit_ver_name in that file. It will tell which version of the JInitiator is being used.

47. What is reports server?

Reports server is also a component of the middle tier and is hosted in the same node of the concurrent processing server. Reports server is used to produce business intelligence reports. Report server is started by executable rwmts60 which is located at $ORACLE_HOME/bin

48. How can you check from the operating system whether the reports server is up and running?

Reports server can be checked from operating system by querying for the process rwmts60. You can check the same using the following command.

ps -ef | grep rwmts60

49. How can you compile a report manually?

You can do the same using the adrepgen utility as shown below. adrepgen apps/<apps_passwd> source = $PRODUCT_TOP/srw/filename.rdf dest=$PRODUCT_TOP/srw/filename.rdf stype=rdffile dtype=rdffile logfile=<path_of_log> overwrite=yes batch=yes dunit=character

50. What is discoverer and why it is used?

Discoverer is an intuitive ad hoc query, reporting, analysis, and Web-publishing tool that empowers business users at all levels of the organization to gain immediate access to information from data marts, data warehouses, online transaction processing systems and Oracle e-business suite. The discoverer server comprises Oracle Discoverer 4i, a key component of the Oracle9i Application Server (9iAS). Discoverer 4i is tightly integrated with Oracle Applications which allow users to employ Discoverer to analyze data from selected business areas in human resources, purchasing, process manufacturing, financials and other products. The discoverer server complements the reports server by allowing performance of ad hoc queries and analysis of the resulting query output. It also allows users to perform projections based on possible changes to the business environment or other strategic factors.

51. How can you start the discoverer server?

Discoverer start script addisctl.sh is available in the $OAD_TOP/admin/scripts/$CONTEXT_NAME location. Alternatively, you can also use the startall.sh script located at $ORACLE_HOME/discwb4/util directory.

52. What is the product directory in the APPL_TOP and what is the importance of the same?

For each product there is a separate directory in the APPL_TOP. There are more than two hundred products in the 11.5.10 release. The product directories are named with the product's standard abbreviation like bis for Business Intelligence System, ec for e-commerce.

The product files are stored in the product directories.

<Prod_Top> refers to <APPL_TOP>/<prod>/Version. For example $FND_TOP=$APPL_TOP/fnd/11.5.0.

Under each product top there are a large number of directories. If we go to FND_TOP directory, we will see the following directories.

(appmgr01) emstestappl - bash $ cd $FND_TOP

(appmgr01) 11.5.0 - bash $ pwd

/slot01/appmgr/emstestappl/fnd/11.5.0

(appmgr01) 11.5.0 - bash $ ls

3rdparty fndenv.env html lib media patch secure xml

admin forms include log mesg reports sql driver

bin help java mds out resource usrxit

(appmgr01) 11.5.0 - bash $

53. What are the important configuration files available in APPL_TOP?

Following are the important configuration files available in the APPL_TOP.

APPLSYS.env/APPSORA.env

Adovars.env

SID.xml

Adconfig.txt

Adjareas.txt

Topfile.txt

Appsweb.cfg

Hostname_SID.dbc

Adpltfrm.txt

Adjborg.txt

Adjborg2.txt

54. What is the significance of the appsweb.cgf file and where is it located?

This file defines the parameter values used by forms Web CGI. This is the main configuration file used by the forms. This file contains the following details:

- Forms Server Name, ServerPort, DomainName
- Database Connection Parameters
- JInitiator Version

This file is located at $OA_HTML/bin.

55. What is the significance of the DBC file and where is it located?

The DBC stands for database connection. This is the file which is responsible for establishing a connection between the database and the APPL_TOP. The DBC file stores all the information for successful connection to the database. The DBC file contains the values of GWYUID, FNDNAM, and TWO_TASK & GUEST_USER_PWD.

GWYUID stands for Gateway User ID and should have APPLSYSPUB/PUB as User ID/Password.

The default User ID/Password for Oracle Applications is guest/guest, guest/oracle, oracle/guest. This User ID/ Password should match with the record available in the fnd_profile_options table.

The location of this file is $FND_TOP/secure.

56. What is the significance of GWYUID?

It is used to connect to database by thick clients.

57. What is the difference between GWYUID and GUEST_USER_PWD?

GWYUID is used by thick clients to connect to the database. For example, forms uses the GWYUID to get connected. Whenever a new forms connection is established, it uses

APPLSYSPUB/PUB to authenticate the session, whereas GUEST_USER_PWD (Guest/Oracle) is used by JDBC thin client.

58. If you go to the FND_TOP/secure directory, you can see lots of DBC files located there. How do you find which one is used by the application system?

To find out which DBC file is used by the application system you can query for the profile Applications Database ID. If the profile name is SID then SID.dbc is used by the application.

59. What is the significance of the admin directory in the APPL_TOP?

The $APPL_TOP/admin directory contains the scripts and the files which are used by the AD utilities. This directory also contains the log and output files created during patching and running of ad utilities. Following are the important files in the $APPL_TOP/admin directory.

- <sid>.xml — This is the context file which is used by the Oracle Applications
- adovars.env — This is an important configuration file about which we have already discussed
- <sid>/log — This directory contains all the logfiles which are generating during patching or by the running of Ad utilities
- <sid>/out — This directory contains all the output files
- Text files — This directory contains a large number of text files which contains various information about the application system and are referred during autopatch

60. How can you change the password of the application users?

The password of the application users as well as the password of all the schemas including apps can be changed using the FNDCPASS utility. For running the FNDCPASS, you need to have the system and the apps password. FNDCPASS is run in the following manner:

FNDCPASS apps/apps 0 Y system/manager SYSTEM APPLSYS WELCOME

FNDCPASS apps/apps 0 Y system/manager ORACLE GL GL1

FNDCPASS apps/apps 0 Y system/manager USER VISION WELCOME

61. What is '0' and 'Y' in flag in FND executables like FNDCPASS, FNDLOAD?

'0' means the request id. Since the request is not submitted via the Concurrent Request submission forms, request id zero is assigned to it.

'Y' indicates the method of invocation. It's invoked directly from the operating system and not through the concurrent request.

62. What are the tables which store the information about the various application users and their passwords?

Two tables—FND_USERS and FND_ORACLE_USERID—store the information about the application users and their passwords.

63. How can you delete an application user?

You can't delete an application user but you can put the end date the application user making the user inactive.

64. In case of a multi-node installation, how can you check which service is being run from which node?

There are two ways to find the same information.

You can open the CONTEXT_FILE in the APPL_TOP/admin and check the information.

You can check for the FND_NODES table and check the column, SUPPORT_CP (for Concurrent Manager) SUPPORT_FORMS (for forms server), SUPPPORT_WEB (Web server), SUPPORT_ADMIN (admin server), and SUPPORT_DB for database tier.

65. What is OATM and what is its significance?

OATM refers to the Oracle Applications tablespace model. In the previous releases of Oracle Applications, there were two tablespaces for each product. One was for data and the other was for the index and there use to be a lot of overhead in managing all the tablespaces. The new tablespace model replaces the old tablespace model by 12 tablespaces making it lot easier to manage the tablespaces.

66. Is apps password stored in any flat file outside database?

Yes the apps password file is stored in the file called wbdbr.app located at $IAS_ORACLE_HOME/Apache/modplsql/cfg.

67. Where are all the middle tier start/stop scripts located?

The scripts for managing the middle tiers are located in COMMON_TOP/admin/scripts/<sid> directory. For running these scripts, login to the application tier as the owner of the application file system and source the environment using the environment <sid>.env located in the $APPL_TOP. All the scripts create a log file which shows the status of the server. The log file is written in the directory $COMMON_TOP/admin/log/<sid>. Each component of the middle tier has a separate log file.

68. What is the script for the start/stop of Apache?

The Apache server can be started with the script adapcctl.sh. The parameters that accepts is start, stop, and status.

adapcctl.sh { start | stop | status }

The Apache startup script is customized for the Oracle Applications in such a way that it takes of starting the Jserv, modplsql and the TCF socket server automatically once the apache is started.

The log file which is created by the script is adapcctl.txt and it is located at the location of the log file.

69. What is the script for starting/stopping the forms server?

The forms server can be controlled with the script adfrmctl.sh which is located at the common locations of all the scripts viz $COMMON_TOP/admin/scripts/<sid>. The forms server can be started/stopped in the following way.

adfrmctl.sh { stop |start | status }

The log file which is created by the scripts is f60svrm.txt available at the common location of the log files.

Alternatively, the forms server can also be started manually without using the scripts with the f60ctl executable which is located at $ORACLE_HOME/bin. This is 8.0.6 Oracle Home and should not be confused with the Oracle Home of the database server.

The forms server can be started manually in the following way.

f60ctl start port=<port name> mode=socket exe=f60webmx logfile=/location of logfile.

70. How you can start the reports server?

Reports server can be controlled with a script adrepctl.sh. It uses the executable FNDSVCRG which is located at $FND_TOP/bin. The default name of the reports server log file is rep60_<sid>.txt and is located at same place along with the log files of the other components of the middle tier.

Reports server can be controlled by

adrepctl.sh { start | stop | status }

71. How you can start/stop all the middle tier components at one go?

For starting and stopping all the middle tiers, Oracle provides two different scripts which take care of starting and stopping all the middle tiers at one go.

For starting all the middle tiers, the script is adstrtal.sh. It takes the apps user id and apps password as parameters.

adstrtal.sh <appsusername/appspassword>

Similarly, for stopping all the middle tiers at one go, the script is adstpal.sh. This also takes the apps user id and apps password as parameters.

adstpall.sh <appsusername/appspassword>

Both these scripts create a log file in which it contains detailed information. The logfile name is in the following format <Month><Date><Hour><Minute>.log

It gives a formatted report in the log file with the details of which components are started, which are already running, which are disabled and which are not running.

2
Installation

1. What is the minimum disk space requirement for installing Oracle Applications?

The approximate file sizes in a single-node installation are:

- Application tier file system—26 GB (includes iAS/8.0.6 ORACLE_HOME COMMON_TOP, and APPL_TOP)
- Database tier file system (fresh install with a production database)—31 GB
- Database tier file system (fresh install with a Vision Demo database)—65 GB
- Total space for a single node system, not including stage area, is 57 GB for a fresh install with a production database, and 91 GB for a fresh install with a Vision Demo database.

2. How much stage area is required for RapidInstall?

To run RapidInstall from a stage area, you need at least 24 GB to accommodate the files.

3. How much space an additional language needs?

To install an additional language, it needs approximately around 10 GB space.

4. Do I need to install any other software before starting the RapidInstall?

Before installing Oracle Applications, the JDK needs to be installed. The version of JDK which needs to be installed depends on which version of Oracle Applications you want to install. The latest 11.5.10 release of Oracle Applications needs JDK1.4.2. Apart from JDK, you must have perl 5.0053 installed and which should be there in your PATH. If you don't have perl installed, download the same from www.perl.com.

5. Can I start the RapidInstall with any user?

RapidInstall needs to be started only with the root user. It can also be started with any other user as well, but that is not recommended as you have two different users—one for databse and other for application file system.

6. How many operating system users I need for Installing Oracle Applications?

Oracle recommends that you should have two Unix users for Installing Oracle Applications—one Oracle user (Oracle) who owns the file system of the database and one application (applmgr) user who owns the application file system.

7. What are the individual disks included in the Release 11i software bundle?

The 11.5.10 software comes in DVD format. The individual disks included in the Release 11*i* software bundle are labeled as follows:

- Start Here—Disk 1
- APPL_TOP—Disk *n*
- RDBMS—Disk *n*
- Tools—Disk *n*
- Databases—Disk *n*

8. Is the NLS software included with the RapidInstall DVD bundle?

No, the NLS software is not included with the RapidInstall bundle.You need to order the NLS supplement software separately for each additional language which you want to install along with Oracle Applications.

9. How do I create the stage area of the RapidInstall?

For creating a stage area, the script adautostg.pl needs to be run as follows:

```
$ cd /mnt/cdrom/Disk1/rapidwiz
$ perl adautostg.pl
```

10. How many directories are there in the stage area of Oracle Applications?

The following six directories are there in the stage area of Oracle Applications.

- StartCD
- oraApps
- oraDB
- oraiAS
- oraAppDB
- oraNLS (Optional only if you have a NLS Software)

11. What pre-install checks should I make to ensure a successful installation?

- Verify the correct users and groups have been created, as documented in installing Oracle Applications.
- Verify the required disk space is available, as documented in installing Oracle Applications.

 - Verify the file system base install directories have write access granted to the user that will own the software (on UNIX the RapidInstall Wizard may be run as root but the install runs as the user that will own the software, therefore this user must have write access to the base install directories).
- Verify the required ports are available for the installation.
- Verify system parameters are sufficient for the Oracle software (especially the database) to run.
- Verify that all the OS patches have been applied as per Oracle documentation.

12. What is a single node installation?

Single node installation is the one in which all the servers (concurrent processing, forms, Web, reports), the database and all product directories are installed on a single node. In other words, in single node installation the entire Oracle Applications are installed on a single server.

13. Where is a single node installation generally used?

The single node installation is generally used for smaller installations and also used for demonstration purpose.

14. What is an express configuration?

Express configuration installs a fully configured single node system with either a fresh database or Vision Demo database. Only a few basic parameters such as database name, top level install directories and port settings needs to be specified in this and express configuring take care of installing Oracle Applications without any user intervention.

15. What is configuration file and why is it used?

During installation RapidInstall asks many questions from the user. It saves all the configuration parameters you enter in a new configuration file (config.txt) which it uses to configure the system for the new installation. In case the installation fails the same configuration file can be used for restarting the installation without answering all the questions again from the scratch. For multi-node installation, this configuration file is used for the installation in other nodes.

16. I have started RapidInstall but nothing is coming in the screen. What could be the reason?

The display might not be set properly. Set the display and start RapidInstall again.

17. What is a multi-node installation?

A multi-node installation is the one in which the database tier and the application tier are installed across two or more nodes.

18. In a multi-node installation how do I find what services are running from which node?

The context file sid_hostname.xml in $APPL_TOP/admin will have the information about the same. It can also be queried from the table FND_NODES. You can query the following columns—SUPPORT_CP for concurrent manager, SUPPORT_FORMS for forms server, SUPPORT_WEB for the apache host and SUPPORT_ADMIN to know the admin tier.

19. What benefits do I get with multi-node installation?

Multi-node installation distributes the server processes across different servers. For example, in a typical example of multiple node, the database is hosted in one physical server the apache is hosted from some other server, the forms are hosted in some other server, the concurrent manager and reports server is hosted from some other server. This helps in distributing the load across various servers and as a result the overall performance of the application system increases.

20. In case of multi-node installation, I will have multiple APPL_TOP's. How will I manage all the different APPL_TOP's?

In earlier releases of the Oracle Applications, this problem was there. In case of patching, patching needs to be done from all the different nodes of the APPL_TOP. But with the introduction of the concept of shared APPL_TOP, this problem has been resolved.

21. What is Shared APPL_TOP and how does it help in case of multi-node installation?

In case of multi-node installation, various components of the middle tiers are hosted across different physical servers. Shared APPL_TOP means the APPL_TOP will be installed only in one of the physical servers and all the other servers of the application tier will share the file system of the APPL_TOP. Any changes made in the shared APPL_TOP file system are immediately visible on all nodes. This helps a lot in managing the application system. In case of patching, it needs to be done only once as all the servers share the same APPL_TOP. With 11.5.10 release, RapidInstall creates a shared APPL_TOP by default for multi-node installation.

22. What is a shared application tier file system?

In a shared application tier file system installation, the APPL_TOP, the COMMON_TOP, and the applications technology stack (ORACLE_HOMEs) are installed on a shared disk resource mounted to each node in the system. These nodes can be used to provide standard application tier services, such as forms, Web and concurrent processing. Any changes made in the shared application tier file system are immediately visible on all nodes.

23. What operating systems can use the shared APPL_TOP?

All RapidInstall platforms except Windows support a shared application tier infrastructure.

24. Can I share the APPL_TOP across different platforms of operating system?

No, sharing of the APPL_TOP is not possible across different platforms because the binaries and libraries of the application file system are platform specific.

25. As of now I am using two different APPL_TOP. Can I merge the existing APPL_TOPs to go for the shared APPL_TOP model?

Yes, you can merge APPL_TOPs which are spread across different nodes. The metalink document 233428.1. mentions in details about doing the same.

26. What is load balancing?

Load balancing distributes processes for Oracle Applications across multiple nodes. This distribution of the workload improves the performance and enhances scalability. If the load balancing then even if the component is down, the application system continues to work. For example, if Apache load balancing is enabled across two nodes then in case one of the nodes is down, all the incoming connections will automatically be rediricted to the other node.

27. In which servers load balancing can be enabled?

The load balancing can be enabled in the forms server, Web server as well as the concurrent processing server.

28. Which products are installed by default along with RapidInstall?

RapidInstall installs all the products automatically regardless of their licensed status. However, you must register products you have licensed so that they are flagged in the system as active. An active flag marks products for inclusion in patching and other tasks that you will perform to update and maintain your system after the initial installation.

29. How can I tell what is installed and licensed after finishing an install?

The script AD_TOP/sql/adutconf.sql against the APPS user schema will generate a detailed file (adutconf.lst) with information about the database configuration and what products are installed and licensed after the rapid installation process completes.

30. I have already done the installation but forgot to license a product I want to use. Can I license it after the installation?

Yes, licensing can be done after the installation. You can do in two ways.

1. Go to AD_TOP and run the script adlicmgr.sh. This will prompt for the additional products to be licensed.
2. From Oracle Applications Manager go to OAM > License Manager > License additional products.

31. I have already done the installation. Now I want to add an additional language. Is it possible?

Yes, it's possible to add a separate language after the installation. For this, you need to make the language as active from Oracle Applications Manager and need to download and install the NLS software.

32. I don't want to use the defaults port that's being used by RapidInstall. What options do I have for changing the ports to some other value?

There are two options for assigning different ports rather than using the default ports while running Rapid Install.

1. You can use the port pool option with which you can increment all the port values at one go. Say you choose a port pool of 5 then all your port values will be incremented by 5 from the default value.
2. You can use the Advance Edit button for assigning the ports of your choice but make sure that the ports which you are assigning are not in use.

33. What are the pre-install checks performed by RapidInstall?

The RapidInstall takes care of the following checks.

1. Port availability: The port you have selected is available or clashing with some existing port.
2. Port uniqueness: There is no duplicate defined port for the processes.
3. File space check: It ensures whether the file system have sufficient space for a smooth installation.
4. OS Patch Check: It ensures that the right operating system patches are there or not.
5. Operating system check: It checks the operating system.
6. File system check: It checks whether the files are mounted properly and have correct permission.
7. Host/domain check: It verifies the hostname and the domain name.

8. System utilities check: It checks whether the linking utilities like make, ld and cc are available or not.
9. OS user and group check: It checks that the OS user exists and the OS user is a part of correct group.

34. How much time does RapidInstall normally take?

RapidInstall approximately takes around 5 – 6 hours to complete in a single node.

35. Once the installation is done, what checks RapidInstall does to ensure that the installation is successful?

RapidInstall checks the following to ensure the installation is successful.

1. Database availability check: The database is up and running
2. Environment file check: Checks whether the environment file is created properly
3. DBC file check: The DBC file has been created (location $FND_TOP/secure)
4. HTTP check: Checks if the apache is up and running
5. JSP check: Checks if the JSPs are working fine
6. PHP check: Checks if the PHPs are working fine

36. Where are RapidInstall log files written?

RapidInstall log files for Application Tier are located under $APPL_TOP/admin/<SID>_<hostname>/log.

The Log files for database tier are located under $ORACLE_HOME/appsutil/log/<SID>_<hostname>

The log file is of the following format XXXXXXX.log. Where XXXXXXXX = MMDDHHMM - date and time of run

37. What information is written in the log files of the RapidInstall of db and application tier?

In the db tier, the RapidInstall log file contains the following information:

- Rapid wizard version
- Date and time install session started
- Rapid wizard source location
- Command line arguments for this execution
- Location of configuration file
- Install session information:
  - ❑ Host name
  - ❑ Host operating system
  - ❑ User running install
- Results of:
  - ❑ Host name
  - ❑ Port availability check
  - ❑ Operating system check
  - ❑ Port uniqueness check
  - ❑ File system check
  - ❑ File space check
  - ❑ Host/domain check
  - ❑ OS patch checks
  - ❑ System utilities check
- Results of the actual installation:
  - ❑ Instantiation drivers
  - ❑ XML file creation
  - ❑ Control file creation
  - ❑ ADX database utility

The application tier log file contains the following information:

- Results of the actual Installation
- Instantiation drivers
- XML creation
- Control file creation
- ADX database utility
- Results of the post install checks
- Database availability check
- Environment file check
- DBC file check
- HTTP check
- JSP check
- PHP check
- 806infrun.log - Windows only - Updating Registry with Tools 8.0.6 ORACLE_HOME information
- iasinfrun.log - Windows only - Updating Registry with Tools iAS ORACLE_HOME information
- iASInstall.log - Information on unzipping stages for oraiAS - Tools 8.0.6 and iAS Techstack
- installAppl.log - Information on unzipping stages for oraApps - APPL_TOP
- installiasinf.log - Information on creating the Registry update .inf files

3
Forms

1. **How do I check from the server if the forms server is running or not?**

   Check for the process f60ctl. If the process is running it means the forms are up and running.

2. **How do I change the port of the forms server?**

   Modify the file appsweb.cgf which is available at $OA_HTML/bin

3. **How do I enable FRD (Forms Runtime Diagnostics)?**

   For enabling FRD, login to forms as sysdmin. Then add "&record=collect&log=" without the quotes to the profile option ICX%FORMS%LAUNCHER.

   The FRD can also be enabled by appending the same on the forms URL play=&record=collect&log=/tmp/form1.frd

   For example, if the forms URL is

   http://ap6105rt.us.oracle.com:8012/dev60cgi/f60cgi?config=SCMTST1

   Then add the following in the URL.

   http://ap6105rt.us.oracle.com:8012/dev60cgi/f60cgi?config=SCMTST1play=&record=collect&log=/tmp/form1.frd

4. How do you relink the f60webmx executable?

It can done from the command line by using the syntax adrelink.sh force=y "fnd f60webmx"

5. My forms server is up and running but while connecting to the forms I am getting the error "Your connection to the server was interrupted. This can be due to a result of network error, or a failure on the server. You will need to reestablish your session", what do I do?

Relink the f60webmx and then bounce the forms server.

6. What is FORMS60_TIMEOUT?

This is an environment setting which refers to the maximum idle time before f60webmx shuts down. This will only terminate an idle middle tier process.

7. How do I generate an FMB file manually?

It can be generated from the command line using the following command:

f60gen module=form_name.fmb userid=apps/apps output_file=form_name.fmx module_type=form batch=yes compile_all=special

8. How can I generate a PLL file manually?

It can be generated from the command line using the following command:

f60gen module=library_name.pll userid=apps/apps module_type=library batch=yes compile_all=special

9. How can I generate an MMB file manually?

It can be generated from the command line using the following command:

f60gen module=FNDMENU.mmb userid=apps/apps output_file=FNDMENU.mmx module_type=menu batch=yes compile_all=special

10. What are important files related to forms?

- adfmcctl.sh—This script starts and stops the forms metric client for apps instance located in $COMMON_TOP/admin/scripts. It uses the forms d2lc60 executable to accomplish this.
- adfmsctl.sh—This script starts and stop the forms metric server for apps instance located in $COMMON_TOP/admin/scripts. It uses the forms d2ls60 executable to accomplish this.
- adfrmctl.sh—This script starts and stops the forms server listener located in $COMMON_TOP/admin/scripts,. It calls the f60ctl found in $ORACLE_HOME/6iserver/bin of IAS.
- appsweb.cfg—This file defines parameter values used by the forms web CGI located in $OA_HTML/html/bin. It has the details of the forms server port, host, domain etc.
- appsbase.html—This is the default HTML file for starting an applet using JInitiator and is located in $OA_HTML/<language>
- d2lc60.txt—This is the forms metric client log file, located in $COMMON_TOP/admin/install
- d2ls60.txt—This is the forms metric server log file, located in $COMMON_TOP/admin/install
- f60svrm.txt—This is the adfrmctl.sh log file located in $COMMON_TOP/admin/install. This is not the same as the forms server log file which not only logs start up and shut down info but also client connectivity. For example, which client IP is associated with which f60webmx process and debug stack trace info.

- OracleApplications.dat—This file determines the path Oracle Apps uses to find their icons and is located in $JAVA_TOP/oracle/apps/fnd/formsClient

11. I am not able to launch the forms through the php. It's simply hanging however I am able to launch the direct forms, how should I fix this?

If you are not able to launch the forms then check for profile ICX: Forms Launcher system profile. Set properly the forms URL here and you should be able to launch the forms.

12. What is the ICX: forms launcher system profile is used for?

This profile option is used by the self service Web applications personal home page (also known as ICX) to determine the base URL needed to launch an application, which in this case is a forms application.

13. What should ICX: forms launcher be set to?

ICX: forms launcher is set to http://hostname:port/dev60cgi/f60cgi? You can optionally add some parameters to this URL to enable tracing.

14. What is FORMS60_CATCHTERM?

FORMS60_CATCHTERM is an environment setting that enables or disables the forms abnormal termination handler which catches middle tier crashes and cleans up by removing temp files, closing db connections and writing diagnostic info to the dump file or the forms server log file.

15. How do you determine version information about a Oracle Applications form?

From the Oracle Applications, open the form whose version you want to know. Go to the menu bar, select Help>About Oracle Applications. Near the bottom of the information screen, you will find a heading of "FORMS". Under this heading you will find the name and version information of the currently selected form.

16. **How do you enable tracing for the forms session and where is the trace file located?**

You can start the tracing for the particular forms session by going to the menu bar of the Oracle Applications forms session and by selecting Tools and then Trace Enable. Once you click Enable it will tell you the full path and name of the trace file. It's normally located in the udump location of the database server.

17. **I want to launch the direct forms for debugging but when I try to launch the direct forms I get the error, "This application server is not authorized to access this database." How can I launch the direct forms?**

By default the launch of direct forms is not supported in Oracle Applications. Still if you want to launch the forms directory then you must set the security off for doing the same. The direct forms can be accessed using the URL given below.

http://<Apache hostname>.<domain>:<Web Port>/dev60cgi/f60cgi

The following command is used for turning the authentication off java oracle.apps.fnd.security.AdminAppServer apps/apps AUTHENTICATION OFF DBC=<name of dbc file>

Once the authentication is set to off then the direct forms URL can be accessed.

18. After logging to the forms you are getting the error—the Menu compilation has failed or Oracle Error there is no valid responsibility available. How will you troubleshoot the same?

If you are getting the errors like this it means that the system has not been completely taken out of the maintenance mode or it is still there in the maintenance mode. Once the system is out of the maintenance mode you will be able to login.

19. When the forms are being launched you can see a yellow bar in the bottom. How to fix the same?

Regenerate the JAR files using adadmin. The problem will be fixed.

20. What is the difference between the forms running in socket mode and servlet mode?

If the forms are run in the socket mode, there will be a dedicated connection between the client desktop and the forms server whereas when the forms are started in the servlet mode, the forms request are processed by the Jserv.

21. How do I find whether the forms are running in servlet mode or in socket mode?

For checking the same, query the f60 process. It will reply in which mode the forms is running.

22. How do I change from the socket to servlet mode and vice versa?

For doing the same, login to the Oracle Applications manager and follow the navigation >Site Map > Autoconfig. From there, you will be able to change from socket mode to servlet mode and vice versa. You have to run autoconfig from the backend and bounce the forms server after doing the same.

4
Concurrent Manager

1. What is concurrent manager?

When an Oracle Applications user submits a request to run a program, it's called concurrent request. Concurrent manager are the programs, which are responsible for running the concurrent requests. When a user submits a report to be run as a concurrent request, the job enters in a request queue. Concurrent managers continuously read request from this master queue and run the requests based on the request's schedule, priority, and compatibility rules. Concurrent managers run in background and they take care of initiating and completing the concurrent requests.

2. What are the different types of concurrent manager?

Oracle Applications consist of several types of concurrent managers. The important ones are internal manager, standard manager and conflict resolution manager. Apart from these, you can define your own custom concurrent manager.

3. What is an internal concurrent manager?

The internal manager is the one which is responsible for controlling all other concurrent managers. Its main task is to ensure that all other concurrent managers are up and running.

The internal concurrent manager starts, sets the number of active processes, monitors and terminates all other concurrent processes through requests made to the service manager, including restarting any failed processes. The internal concurrent manager also starts and stops, and restarts the service manager for each node.

4. What is conflict resolution manager?

The conflict resolution manager takes care of resolving the program incompatibilities and checks if a request in queue can be run in parallel with the running request. It also takes care of resolving the program incompatibilities. If a program is identified as run alone, then the conflict resolution manager prevents the concurrent managers from starting other programs in the same conflict domain.

When a program lists other programs as being incompatible with it, the conflict resolution manager prevents the program from starting until any incompatible programs in the same domain have completed running.

5. What is a standard manager?

The standard manager is the master concurrent manager. This manager is always running and it can take care of processing any concurrent request. It has no specialization rules. This manager runs 24 hours a day for the whole year. The definition of this manager should never be altered. In case if you alter the definition of the standard manager and you have not defined additional managers to run your requests, some of the programs may not run in a proper way.

6. How do I enable/disable the conflict resolution manager?

There is a system profile option "Concurrent: Use ICM". The default value of this profile option is No which allows the conflict resolution manager to be started. Setting the same to Yes will cause the conflict resolution manager to be shutdown and the internal concurrent manager will take care of the conflict resolution duties. Using the internal concurrent manager to resolve the conflicts is not recommended.

7. What are the different ways to start concurrent manager?

Concurrent manager can be started using the script adcmctl.sh located at the locations of the scripts or with the startmgr utility located at $FND_TOP/bin.

8. What are the different ways to stop concurrent manager?

Concurrent manager can be stopped using the script adcmctl.sh. It can also be stopped using the Concsub utility. From the operating system, the concurrent manager can be stopped by querying the FNDLIBR process and killing the same.

9. In administer concurrent manager form there are two columns labeled as actual and target. What are these columns and what is their significance?

Target column lists the number of processes that should be running for each manager for this particular workshift. Actual column lists the number of processes that are actually running. If the actual column is zero, there are no processes running for this manager. If the target column is zero, then either a workshift has not been assigned to this manager, or the current workshift does not specify any target processes. If the target column is not zero, then the manager processes have either failed to start up, or has gone down.

10. How do I run/schedule a concurrent request from operating system level without logging into the applications?

A concurrent request can be scheduled/run from the operating system using the CONCSUB utility. CONCSUB means Concurrent Submit.

11. What are the different ways to check if concurrent manager (CM) is running or not?

There are a couple of ways through which one can check if the CM is running or not. From the operating system, it can be checked by querying the FNDLIBR process. From the forms, it can be checked from the Navigation > Concurrent > Manager >Administer. It can be also checked using the scripts adcmctl.sh status and finally it can also be checked from Oracle Applications Manager.

12. What is the default location of the concurrent manager logfiles?

The concurrent manager log files can be located in one of the following places:

1. If the environment variable $APPLCSF is set, the default location is $APPLCSF/$APPLLOG
2. If the environment variable $APPLCSF is not set, the logs go to $FND_TOP/$APPLLOG

13. I have submitted a request and it's showing the status inactive/no manager. Concurrent manager is up and running and the request are being picked after some time. What could be the reason for the same?

If the concurrent manager is up and running and the request goes to the status inactive/no manager for some time it means that cache cycle is less. Cache size is set on the Concurrent> Manager> Define form. Basically, this regulates how many requests a manager will pick up for each sleep cycle. The solution is either to increase the cache size of the manager or increase the actual number of the manager process. The manager could be standard manager or any other manager for which the issue is coming.

14. I have submitted a request, it has gone to pending standby status for a long time whereas other requests are getting completed normally without any issues. What could be the reasons?

If any particular request is going to pending standby status and others are getting completed, it means that either it is waiting for the output of some other request or is conflicting with some other request. If the request is conflicting, check the queue of the conflict resolution manager for troubleshooting.

15. How do I process more concurrent requests in parallel?

If you want to process more requests simultaneously, there are two ways for the same—one, increase the number of the target process for the manager and second, change the cache size of the concurrent manager.

16. When do the tables FND_CONCURRENT_REQUESTS and FND_CONCURRENT_PROCESS need to be purged?

When the tables reach 20,000 rows, the performance begins to diminish. You may want to run purge concurrent request on a regular basis, depending on the amount of requests being run.

17. What are the concurrent request log file and output file naming conventions?

Request log files: l<request id>.req

Output files: If $APPCPNAM is not set: <username>.<request id>

If $APPCPNAM = REQID: o<request id>.out

If $APPCPNAM = USER: <username>.out

Where: <request id> = The request id of the concurrent request

And: <username> = The id of the user that submitted the request

Manager log files:

ICM log file: Default is std.mgr, can be changed with the mgrname startup parameter

Concurrent manager log: w<XXXXXX>.mgr

Transaction manager log: t<XXXXXX>.mgr

Conflict Resolution manager log: c<XXXXXX>.mgr

Where: <XXXXXX> is the concurrent process id of the manager.

18. What happens when the internal concurrent manager dies? Are all the managers also killed immediately after it?

No, if the internal manager dies, the request continues to run normally except for queue control requests.

19. Does the internal manager run or schedule any request for itself?

No, the internal manager does not run or schedule any requests. It has nothing to do with scheduling requests, or deciding which manager will run a particular request. Its function is only to run 'queue control' requests, which are requests to startup or shutdown other managers. It is responsible for startup and shutdown of the whole concurrent processing facility, and it also monitors the other managers periodically, and restarts them if they should go down. It can also take over the conflict resolution manager's job, and resolve incompatibilities.

20. If the internal manager goes down, do I need to kill all the managers before restarting the internal manager?

No, if the internal manager goes down you need not kill all the managers. You can simply start the internal manager using startmgr.

21. Can I delete concurrent manager?

Yes, you can delete any concurrent manager. For deleting, query for the manager in the defined concurrent manager form and then delete the row.

Deleting the predefined concurrent managers is not recommended and it should never be done. Deletion may cause instability in the system.

22. What is internal monitor?

This manager is used to implement parallel concurrent processing. It monitors whether the ICM is still running, and if the ICM crashes, it will restart it on another node.

23. How do I clean out concurrent manager tables?

For cleaning concurrent manager tables, Oracle provides a script called cmclean.sql.

24. I hit the restart button to start the standard manager but it still doesn't start?

Asking a manager to restart sets the status to restart. The internal concurrent manager will start in the next process monitor session or the next time internal concurrent manager starts. Use activate, to start a manager immediately. Also, when a manager is deactivated manually, the internal concurrent manager will not restart it. You will need to set it to restart, or activate it manually.

25. I tried to stop the concurrent manager using the script adcmctl.sh. I can still see from the operating system that a few FNDLIBR processes are still running and adcmctl.sh is not able to stop the concurrent manager completely. What do I do in this situation?

If you are not able to stop the concurrent manager using the script, query for the FNDLIBR process using the command

ps -ef | grep FNDLIBR

And then kill all the process using the command

Kill –9 <process id>

If there are more than one process of the FNDLIBR, you can kill all of them in one go using the command

Ps –ef | grep FNDLIBR | awk '{ print $2}' | xargs kill –9

26. What are the circumstances in which you need to bounce the concurrent manager?

The following are the situations in which one may need to bounce the concurrent manager.

- When you modify the definition of the printers
- When you modify the environment variables. Say you have changed the APPLTMP and APPLPTMP variable
- When all the requests are pending or hanging

27. What are the reasons a concurrent manager hangs?

The concurrent manager hangs due to many reasons. A few of them are:

- Long running jobs
- The internal manager was activated by someone other than owner of the application system
- The operating system files system is full
- It's not able to create the log file
- You've shut down the internal manager, but actual has a number in it
- The database is hanging may be because the archive log files have filled
- There could be some ORA error that's coming
- Pending/standby requests are too many

28. How can you stop concurrent manager using the CONSCUB utility?

Concurrent manager can be stopped using the CONSCUB utility by the following command:

CONCSUB apps/apps@<dbname> SYSADMIN 'System Administrator' SYSADMIN CONCURRENT FND SHUTDOWN

29. What are the different parameters of the startmgr utility?

The parameters of the startmgr utility is given in the following table.

Parameters	Description	Default
sysmgr	Sqlplus sername/password that owns the foundation tables	Applsys/<passwd>
Mgrname	The name of the Manager	Internal Manager
Log file	The log file of the Manager	$FND_TOP/$APPLLOG/ $mgrname.mgr or $APPLCSF/$APPLLOG/ $mgrname.mgr
Sleep	The number of seconds the ICM should wait before checking new request from the table FND_CON-CURRENT_REQUESTS	60 Seconds
Restart	If the CM goes down abnormally, it will automatically restart the manager. Y = the number of minutes the ICM waits before restarting the manager	N=not to restart after abnormal termination
mailto	MAILTO is a list of users who should receive mail whenever the manager terminates	Current user
printer	The default printer for sending the output files	
diag	This is used for diagnosis. If the CM is started with the parameter diag=y then full diagnostic output is produced in the log file	N
Pmon	The number of sleep cycles ICM will wait before checking failed Managers	20
Quesiz	Number of pmon cycles the ICM waits between times it checks for normal changes in concurrent manager operation. Normal changes include the start or end of a work shift and changes to the concurrent manager definitions entered in the Define Concurrent Manager form. (Default 1)	1

30. What exactly happens when a concurrent request is submitted?

Once a concurrent request is submitted by the user, the table FND_CONCURRENT_REQUESTS is automatically updated with the details of the request. The table is also updated with the information about the schedule of the concurrent request whether it's immediately scheduled or scheduled at a fixed time. Once the request is scheduled to run the concurrent manager checks the FND_CONCURRENT_REQUESTS table to find out if the request is incompatible with any other request. If the request is incompatible then the conflict resolution manager takes care of the request and finds out what are the incompatibilities and resolves them. If there are no incompatibilities, it's checked whether any special manager is there to take care of this request. If there is any special manager to take care of this request then it goes to the queue of that manager else the standard manager takes care of the same. Once the request is processed, the FND_CONCURRENT_REQUESTS table is updated with the status.

31. In the administer concurrent manager form, what is the significance of the terminate button?

The terminate button is used to terminate any concurrent manager. When you terminate internal manager, all the managers automatically get deactivated and all the running requests are terminated. If you want to terminate a particular manager, select the manager and click the terminate button. The status of the manager changes to deactivate after a few seconds and all the requests processed by that manager are immediately terminated. Once a manager is terminated, it doesn't restart automatically. You have to manually restart it using the restart button.

32. In administer concurrent manager form, what is the significance of the deactivate button and how can you deactivate a manager from there?

For deactivating a particular manager, select the manager and press the deactivate button. In case of deactivation, all the requests processed by the manager are allowed to complete before the manager shuts down. If you deactivated the internal manager, all the managers automatically get deactivated but all the running requests are allowed to complete before the manager is shut down. This is the only difference between termination and deactivation. In termination, all the running requests are terminated immediately whereas in case of deactivation all the running requests are allowed to complete first.

33. In administer concurrent manager form, what is the significance of the verify button and for which managers it's available?

The verify button becomes enable only when you select the internal manager. One of the functions of the internal manager is to monitor the processes of each concurrent manager. The process of monitoring the other concurrent manager by internal manager is known as the PMON cycle. When you click the verify button you can force the process monitoring or the PMON activity to occur. The verfiy button is also available for the conflict resolution manager which checks for the program incompatibilities.

34. What is parallel concurrent processing and what is the significance of the same?

Parallel concurrent processing is the way to distribute concurrent managers across multiple nodes in a cluster, massively parallel, or networked environment. It helps in distributing the load across multiple nodes thereby fully utilizing the hardware resource.

The following are the advantages of the parallel concurrent processing.

Load Distribution	Since the concurrent processing is distributed among multiple servers, as a result the load is distributed across various nodes which results in high performance.
Fault Tolerance	When a node fails, the concurrent processes continues to run on other nodes, as a result the work is not hampered.
Single Point of Control	The ability to administer concurrent managers running on multiple nodes from any node in a cluster, massively parallel, or networked environment.

35. Explain briefly how parallel concurrent processing works.

In case of parallel concurrent processing, all the managers are assigned a primary and a secondary node. The managers are started in their primary node by default. In case of node failure or Oracle instance failure, all the concurrent managers on that node are switched to their secondary nodes. Once the primary node is available again the concurrent managers on the secondary nodes are migrated back to the primary node. During the migration process, a manager may be spread across both primary and secondary nodes.

In case of parallel concurrent processing, it may happen that in a node where parallel concurrent processing is configured, the Oracle instance may or may not be running. The node which is not running Oracle, the concurrent managers connects via Net8 to a node which is running Oracle.

The internal concurrent manager can run on any node, and can activate and deactivate concurrent managers on all nodes. Since the internal concurrent manager must be active at all times, it needs high fault tolerance. To provide this fault tolerance, parallel concurrent processing uses internal monitor processes. The job of the internal monitor process is to constantly monitor the internal manager and start it when it fails. Only one internal monitor process can be active on a single node. You decide which nodes have an internal monitor process when you configure your system. You can also assign each internal monitor process a primary and a secondary node to ensure fail over protection. Internal monitor processes, like concurrent managers, can be assigned work shifts, and are activated and deactivated by the internal concurrent manager.

The concurrent log and output files from requests that run on any node are accessible online from any other node. Users need not log onto a node to view the log and output files from requests running on that node.

36. Where can I define the primary and the secondary nodes for the concurrent manager from?

For defining the primary and secondary nodes of each manager, you need to launch forms with system administer and need to navigate the Concurrent > Manager > Define form. Query for the manager in which you want to define the primary and secondry node. In this screen, put the values for the primary and the secondary nodes and save.

37. I have defined for nodes of the concurrent manager. Now do I need to start the concurrent manager from all the nodes?

No, even if you have defined the concurrent manager in four different nodes you need not start the concurrent manager from all the nodes. You just need to start the concurrent manager from the primary node and GSM takes care of starting the concurrent manager from all the other nodes.

38. My requests are making error out with the error—unable to create temporary files xxxxx.tmp. How do I fix it?

This issue normally comes if the values of $APPLTMP, $APPLPTMP in the APPL_TOP and the utl_file_dir parameter of the database are not in sync. All the three variables should be exactly the same. If these issues come, change the values to make all these three in sync. If you change the values in the APPSORA.env, you need to bounce the concurrent manager for the changes to get effected. In case if you change the values of the init.ora, you need to bounce the database to reflect the changes. (Of course you need to bounce the application tier also if you are bouncing the database.)

39. The user comes to you saying that the request is taking a lot of time to complete. What will be your approach for debugging it?

You can do the following to debug the same.

- You can run a trace on the request id to find the expensive sql's and then tell the developer to fix the same.
- You can check the program incompatibilities in the concurrent request.
- You can check the query which the concurrent program is executing and see if it is creating any locks in the database.

- Many times the users schedule the request to run at a later time.

You can check the parameters with which the request is run. (For example, once a user came saying the request is not printing the output. On checking the possible things, it was realized that he scheduled the request with print copies = 0.)

40. How can you know which trace file is created for the particular request?

You can find out the same using the script given below. The trace will be located in the udump location of the database server.

```
prompt
accept request prompt 'Please enter the
concurrent request id for the appropriate
concurrent program:'
prompt
column traceid format a8
column tracename format a80
column user_concurrent_program_name format
a40
column execname format a15
column enable_trace format a12
set lines 80
set pages 22
set head off

SELECT 'Request id: '||request_id ,
'Trace id: '||oracle_Process_id,
'Trace Flag: '||req.enable_trace,
'Trace Name:
'||dest.value||'
||lower(dbnm.value)||'_ora_'||oracle_process_id||
'.trc',
'Prog. Name:
'||prog.user_concurrent_program_name,
'File Name:
'||execname.execution_file_name||
```

```
execname.subroutine_name ,
'Status :
'||decode(phase_code,'R','Running')
||'-'||decode(status_code,'R','Normal'),
"SID Serial: "||ses.sid||",'||
ses.serial#,
"Module : "||ses.module
from fnd_concurrent_requests req,
v$session ses, v$process proc,
v$parameter dest, v$parameter dbnm,
fnd_concurrent_programs_vl prog,
fnd_executables execname
where req.request_id = &request
and req.oracle_process_id=proc.spid(+)
and proc.addr = ses.paddr(+)
and dest.name='user_dump_dest'
and dbnm.name='db_name'
and req.concurrent_program_id =
prog.concurrent_program_id
and req.program_application_id =
prog.application_id
and prog.application_id =
execname.application_id
and
prog.executable_id=execname.executable_id;
```

41. What are the things that need to be taken care when you define a concurrent program?

When defining a concurrent program the following things need to be taken care.

- Selecting an executable file to run the program
- Choosing the execution method for the program (when defining your executable in define concurrent program executable)
- Defining parameters for the program, if any
- Defining printing information

- Specifying any incompatible program that must not run while the program runs
- Choosing whether to allow users to run this report from the run reports form or from within a form. If the latter option is chosen, the form from which you want to kick-off your program needs to be modified. If the first option is chosen, the program needs to be added to a report security group.

42. How do you schedule concurrent requests?

For scheduling the concurrent requests, you need to click the schedule button while submitting the request. The concurrent program can be scheduled only once, periodically or on some specific days. You can also save this schedule for future reference and can use the same schedule for a different concurrent program by using the option apply a saved schedule. If you don't schedule the request then by default the concurrent requests are submitted immediately.

43. What does the completion option mean at the time of submitting a request?

The completion option refers to what Oracle Applications will do once the request is completed. It can notify people via email, can save the output in a file, can take a print out of the same or simply won't do anything.

44. What is a work shift?

The work shift defines the time for which the concurrent manager is active. You can define some fixed date or time for manager or can make the manager run 24 × 7 making it active all the times. The work shifts are defined by using the work shift form from the following navigation > Concurrent > Manager > Work Shifts.

45. What are the important scripts related to the concurrent managers and what are their locations?

The following SQL scripts located under $FND_TOP/sql are useful when diagnosing concurrent manager problems.

1. afimchk.sql Informs about the status of the ICM and PMON method.
2. afcmstat.sql Lists active manager processes.
3. afrqrun.sql Lists all the running, waiting and terminating requests.
4. afrqwait.sql Lists requests that are constrained and waiting for the ICM to release them.
5. afrqscm.sql Prints log file name of managers that can run a given request. It can be used to check for possible errors when a request stays in pending status. It requires a request id value.
6. afcmcreq.sql Prints the log file name of the manager that processed the request.
7. afrqstat.sql Summary of completed concurrent requests grouped by completion status and execution type. It requires number of days prior to the current date, when to report parameter.
8. afimlock.sql Lists locks that the internal concurrent manager is waiting to get.
9. afcmrrq.sql Lists managers that currently are running a request.

46. What are the things you need to check if you are not able to view the logs of the concurrent manager?

- You need to cross check the TNS entries.
- You need to check the DBC file.
- You need to check if the Aapche/Jserv is running properly.
- You need to check if the connect descriptor is correct.

5
Patching

1. What is the difference between patch, minipack and maintenance pack?

In simple language,

Patch + Patch = Minipack

Mini-pack + Minipack = Maintenance Pack

Patches are created and released by Oracle whenever some new enhancements are made in Oracle Applications or if there is some issue with Oracle Applications. A patch may contain a fix for a single issue or a collection of issues.

During a release cycle, a product combines all the individual patches into a minipack. When these minipacks are combined together into a single patch, it is called a maintenance pack. In earlier release, these minipacks were referred as patch sets and maintenance packs were referred as release updates.

2. What are the different types of driver a patch can have?

A patch can have the following kinds of driver.

- Copy driver known as C driver
- Database driver known as D driver

- Generation drive known as G driver
- Unified driver known as U driver

3. What is a copy driver (C driver) and what does it do?

The copy driver copies all the files that are there in the patch to the APPL_TOP. The copy driver is named as c<patch number>.drv. Apart from copying the files to the APPL_TOP, the copy driver also does the following tasks.

- Copies the files that are there in the patch to the $APPL_TOP.
- Extracts the appropriate files from each product's C library.
- Relinks the Oracle Applications products.
- Regenerates the JAR files and compiles the Java Server Pages (JSP) files.
- Compares the files in the patch with the files in the $APPL_TOP. If the files in the patch are of higher version then only adpatch copies the files from patch to $APPL_TOP.

4. What is a database driver (D driver) and what does it do?

The database driver contains all the commands to change the database object. Just like the copy driver, the database driver is also named as d<patch number>.drv. The database driver applies all the assorted scripts copied by the copy driver to the database. There are many scripts that make changes to the database which are applied by the D driver. Here is the brief description of all the scripts that are run by the D driver.

- It makes a list of all the invalid objects that are there in the database.

- Runs SQL scripts which make changes to the database objects.
- Compiles all the invalid objects that are there in the database.

5. What is a generate driver (G driver) and what does it do?

Just like the copy driver and database driver, the generate driver is also named as g<patch number>.drv . The generate driver regenerates all forms, reports and pl/sql libraries that have been affected by the patch.

6. What is unified driver (U driver) and what does it do?

The unified driver is combination of C, D and G drivers. It performs the acts in the order of C, D and G drivers. For unified driver, the same naming convention follows. It's also named as u<patch number>.drv. It requires only a single execution of AutoPatch.

7. How is a patch applied in an application system?

A patch is applied in using the adpatch utility. It's an interactive utility which prompts for the various details like the patch number, driver details, number of workers, apps password and system password. When all the details are provided, adpatch applies the patch.

8. What exactly happens when a patch is applied? What is the sequence of steps adpatch follows?

The AutoPatch extracts the appropriate files from the product library. It compares the extracted object modules with their corresponding files in the patch directory. If a file in the patch directory is a more recent version than the product's current file, AutoPatch backs up the product's current file into a subdirectory of the patch directory.

Specifically, it backs up

<PROD>_TOP/<subdir(s)>/<old_file_name>

to

<patch_dir>/backup/<env_name>/<appl_top_name>/<prod>/<subdir(s)>/ \

<old_file_name>.

Where <patch_dir> is the patch directory, <env_name> is the Applications Environment name, <appl_top_name> is the APPL_TOP name, and <prod> is the name of the product being patched.

It also replaces each product's outdated files with newer files from the patch directory.

It applies changed Java class files and regenerates JAR files as needed.

It loads the new object modules into the libraries.

It relinks the Oracle Applications products with the Oracle Server.

It runs SQL scripts and exec commands, which change Oracle Applications database objects. By default, AutoPatch does this in parallel.

It copies any specified HTML or media files to their respective destinations.

It generates Oracle Forms files.

It generates Oracle Reports files.

It generates Oracle Graphics files.

It appends a record of how it changed your system to applptch.txt in the $APPL_TOP/admin/<SID> directory

It records summary information of actions actually performed to applpsum.txt located under APPL_TOP/admin.

It updates the various ad tables like ad_applied_patches, ad_bugs with the status of the patch.

9. I want to apply a couple of patches in my application system. Can I apply all the patches together?

No. You can't apply all the patches together. You can apply only one patch at a time. If you want to apply multiple patches together, then you can merge all the patches together using the merge patch utility and can apply the merged patch at one go.

10. How can I apply a patch in a non-interactive manner?

You can apply a patch in a non-interactive manner using a patch defaults file. The defaults file stores all the information that is normally asked by the adpatch and uses them to apply the patch in a non-interactive manner.

11. How do I create a defaults file for applying a patch in a non-interactive manner?

For creating the defaults file for the first time we need to give the following at the prompt.

(appmgr01) bash $ adpatch\ defaultsfile=$APPL_TOP/admin/$TWO_TASK/def.txt

This will prompt all the questions that are normally asked during interactive patching. Answer all the questions and when asked for the directory where your patch has been unloaded, enter an abort at the command prompt. This will create a def.txt file at the location specified in the command prompt. Verify whether this defaults file is created properly or not. Once the defaults file is created for the application system, we can run AutoPatch in non interactive way.

12. What is the test mode of adpatch and why is it used?

The test mode is used to determine the action of the patch without actually applying the patch. When the patch is run in test mode it does not perform any action as such but documents the operations it would have performed. In other words, it lists each file it would have copied, generated, executed or relinked. This is used when you want to know what exactly the patch is going to do and what is going to be the impact of the same.

13. How can you apply a patch in the test mode?

You can apply a patch in the test mode by typing adpatch apply=no at the command prompt.

14. Under what circumstances one needs to run a patch in a pre-install mode and how is it run?

Pre-install mode is normally used to update AD utilities before an upgrade to Oracle Applications. This is run from the command prompt by invoking the following command.

Adpatch preinstall=y

15. From release 11.5.10 onwards one needs to put his application system into maintenance mode before applying any patch. How can I apply any patch without putting my application system into maintenance mode?

You can apply a patch without putting the application system into maintenance mode by using the hotpatch option. Type the following from the command line.

adpatch options=hotpatch

16. I was applying a patch and the patch failed. I contacted Oracle support and they advised me to apply one more

patch as a fix and then restart my previously failed patch from the point where it had failed. How do I do that?

If you want to restart your patch from the point where it failed then backup the out and restart directories from the $APPL_TOP/admin/$TWO_TASK. Also take a backup of the FND_INSTALL_PROCESS and AD_DEFERRED _JOBS table from the database and apply the new patch. Once the new patch is applied, put the files that have taken the backup in the place and revert the old table. You should be able to apply the patch from the point where it failed.

17. How can I determine the effects a patch will have on my application system?

You can do the patch impact analysis through the patch wizard in the Oracle Applications Manager. The patch impact analysis feature of patch wizard will give the following details.

- The total number of files in the patch
- The number of files the patch will install
- The products that will have updated files
- The files that will be introduced by the patch
- The files on the target system that will be changed by the patch
- The files with dependencies on patched files

18. I have a two node APPL_TOP. Do I need to apply adpatch from all the nodes?

If you have a shared APPL_TOP which is mounted across both the nodes then you need not apply patches from both the nodes. But if shared APPL_TOP is not enabled and you are maintaining two different APPL_TOP from two different servers then you have to apply the adpatch from both the nodes.

19. **In case of multi-node installation, how do I know which driver file needs to be run from which application server?**

    In case of a multi-node installation, you need to run the C driver from all the nodes as it copies the files that are there in the patch to the APPL_TOP. The D driver needs to be run only once from the admin tier and the G driver needs to be run from the servers where the forms servers are hosted.

20. **How do I know what servers are hosted from which nodes?**

    You can check the same either from the Oracle Application Manager's dashboard or from the context file or from the FND_NODEs table.

21. **In my patch only U driver is there. I tried applying the patch earlier but it failed due to some database issue. I have fixed that issue and now I want only the D and G drivers portions to run and I don't want to run the C driver portion of the patch again. Can I do the same?**

    Yes, you can skip the C driver part from the patch by typing the following at the command prompt

    Adpatch options=nocopyportion.

    Similarly, you can skip the D and G drivers part also by the option nodatabaseportion and nogenerateportion.

22. **While applying patch using adpatch, how can you hide the passwords?**

    You can use adpatch flags=hidepw while applying patches to hide apps or system password.

23. What happens if I apply the driver in the wrong sequence. Say I apply the G driver before the C and D drivers?

The driver always needs to be applied in the C, D and G sequence. If you try to run the G driver before the C driver the patch won't be able to find the forms which the G driver wants to generate, as the C driver has not copied them in the APPL_TOP and hence the patch will fail.

24. What are AutoPatch restart files?

Restart files store information about completed processing in the event of a patch or system failure. They allow AutoPatch, AutoUpgrade, and AD Administration to continue processing at the point where they stopped.

The restart files are located at $APPL_TOP/admin/<SID>/restart.

25. Where do I find the log files of the patch?

The patch log files are located in the $APPL_TOP/admin/$TWO_TASK/log directory. The default name of the patch log file is adpatch.log but it is recommended to change it as patch driver.log in order to identify the patch log easily.

26. What are all the log files which the patch creates?

Running the patch creates the following log files.

- Adpatch.log: It contains the information about the patch run.
- Adpatch.lgi: It contains the other information about the patch run. For example, the files which has not been copied by the adpatch.
- Adrelink.log: It contains the relinking information which the patch does.

- Adworkxx.log: It contains the various workers log.

27. How to find if a patch is applied in an instance or not?

You can query the tables ad_applied_patches to find out if the patches have been applied to the instance or not. You can also check the ad_bugs to find if a patch is applied or not.

28. What is difference between ad_applied_patches and ad_bugs tables for finding the patch information?

The table ad_applied_patches is updated only if the patch is applied by the adpatch utility. If the patch is a part of some other big patch then that information won't be there in the ad_applied_patch as it is not applied using adpatch. But that patch information will be there in ad_bugs. Also, if all the patches are applied using the adpatch utility, that information is also stored in the ad_bugs table.

29. While applying patch, it's showing me "tafnw1" as default APPL_TOP value. What does it mean?

- "t" stands for "tier"
- "a" stands for the "admin" tier
- "f" stands for the "forms" tier
- "n" stands for the "node" tier
- "w" stands for the "Web" tier

30. I was applying a patch and the workers have failed. How do I skip and restart the failed workers?

For this, you need to open a new terminal and invoke the adctrl utility. Choose the eighth options which are generally hidden for skipping and restarting the worker.

31. You were applying a patch and it has failed. What do you do?

If the patch has failed then the first step would be to check the patch log file to find out where exactly it has failed. If the patch fails at D driver or G driver then you should also check the workers log to find out the exact error. Then try to fix the issue. If it is fixed, restart the patching using the adctrl utility.

32. You have applied a patch which brings new files to the APPL_TOP but after applying the patch the users are complaining that they are not able to see the new changes. How do you troubleshoot this?

Check the lgi file of the patch in the log location. You will get some clue whether adpatch has copied or applied that file or not. Else clear the cache from the server and bounce the apache.

33. How do I clear the cache from the server?

In the COMMON_TOP directory, there will a directory starting with _pages. This is the directory where the files are cached in the server. Delete all the files from there for clearing the cache.

34. You have to apply a multiple number of patches. How can you reduce the downtime?

You can reduce the patching time in a number of ways.

- You can merge all the patches into one single patch using admergepatch admrgpch.
- You can choose the max number of the workers which your CPU permits.
- In case you are applying all the patches one by one, you can choose the options nocompiledb nocompilejsp and nolink so that compilation of the invalids object, jsp's and relinking can

be skipped till the last patch is applied. In the last patch you can compile all of them and do the relink.

35. How will you compile JSPs manually?

You can use the script ojspCompile.pl located at $JTF_TOP/admin/scripts to compile JSP files. The syntax for running this is

perl ojspCompile.pl —compile —quiet

36. Is it possible to revert the patch application? Explain in detail how will you revert?

It's not 100% possible to revert the patching. It's always recommended to take the full backup of the database and apply the patch in the test environment at first. In case the patch fails, it's always recommended to revert from the backup. But if the patch is very small and doesn't contain many files then in some cases it's possible to revert the patching application. Adpatch takes a backup of all the files that are there in the APPL_TOP before copying the files from the patch. For reverting the patch action first, a list needs to be made from the log file to find out the files that the patch has copied to the APPL_TOP. Restore all the old files that the adpatch has backed up. Also find out from the patch log which database objects have been created by the patch, drop the objects created by the patch and create those objects using the files that were backed up by adpatch. This is a very risky affair because if the table contains data, it will cause instability in the system. This step should never be performed without the supervision of Oracle support. Similarly for the G driver, the forms should be replaced from the backup which the adpatch has taken and should be manually generated.

37. **Sometimes the adpatch gives a warning like "AutoPatch warning: Skipping product rla (Oracle ID = 710, IGN = 0) (Oracle ID = 710, IGN = 0)". What could be the reason for this error?**

This means that your applprod.txt has more product info than those really installed on the database.

38. **Sometimes the adpatch errors out with the message adogjf() unable to generate jar files under APPL_TOP. How can you fix this issue?**

To fix this issue, open a new terminal and regenerate the product JAR files using adadmin and then restart the patch. Most likely, it will fix the issue. If the issue is still not fixed then create a new certificate using the command "adjkey –initialize" and then regenerate the JAR files.

39. **What is the significance of the FND_INSTALL_PROCESSES table during patching process?**

FND_INSTALL_PROCESSES table is created at the time of the patch applications. It keeps a track of all the files that need to be applied in the application system and which file has been assigned to which worker.

40. **While applying a patch you get this error — This patch has some prerequisites specified, but a "snapshot" of this APPL_TOP's file system has been never taken, thereby rendering it impossible to check for prerequisites. Please take a "snapshot " of this APPL_TOP using "AD Administration" first.
How will you fix this?**

For fixing it, you can take a snapshot of the APPL_TOP using adadmin. It can take up to two hours if you are taking the snapshot of the APPL_TOP for the first time. If you don't want to wait that long then the workaround is to apply the patch using the option "noprereq". From the command prompt type

adpatch options=noprereq

41. What are the various important AD tables and what are their importances?

The important AD tables are given below.

Table	Description
AD_APPL_TOPS	Stores information about all APPL_TOPs utilizing this instance.
AD_APPLIED_PATCHES	Stores information about all distinct updatesapplied
AD_BUGS	Stores information about all distinct bug fixes applied.
AD_FILE_VERSIONS	Stores version information for files.
AD_FILES	Stores information about files in the system.
AD_PATCH_COMMON_ACTIONS	Stores information about actions in update driver files.
AD_PATCH_DRIVER_LANGS	Stores information about the languages included in an update driver file.
AD_PATCH_DRIVER_MINIPKS	Stores information about mini-packs.
AD_PATCH_RUN_BUG_ACTIONS	Stores detailed information about actions applied by an update.
AD_PATCH_RUN_BUGS	Stores information about all bug fixes included in an update, applied or not.
AD_PATCH_RUNS	Stores information about all invocations of AutoPatch for all of the various updates applied.
AD_RELEASES	Stores release information about the Oracle Applications system.

42. When you apply a patch, a view becomes invalid. How do you recreate the view?

Most views are recreated using sql script. These scripts for recreating the views are located in the Product top/patch/115/sql directory. For recreating the view you can grep for the view name in the SQL directory and can find the SQL script which creates the view. You can recreate the view by running that SQL script.

6
Ad Utilities

1. What are Ad utilities?

Ad utilities stand for application DBA utilities. These are a set of tools used for installing, upgrading, maintaining and patching Oracle Applications. There are around 15 Ad utilities, which are shipped along with Oracle Applications.

2. What is maintenance mode and how to enable/disable the same?

Maintenance mode is a feature which is introduced in 11.5.10. For doing any maintenance activity in the application system like applying patches, the maintenance mode needs to be enabled in the application system. It can be enabled/disabled using the adutility adadmin. In the adadmin main menu, there is an option 'Change Maintenance Mode' which is used for changing the maintenance mode.

3. What is the log file location for all the Ad utilities?

The default log file location for all the Ad utilites is $APPL_TOP/admin/$TWO_TASK/log. The log file is in the format <adutility_name>.log. For example the log file of the adadmin will have the name adadmin.log.

4. What is adadmin and why is it used?

Adadmin (Ad administration) is used to perform a number of administrative tasks to maintain the Oracle Applications. Adadmin ensures that Oracle Applications run smoothly.

The Adadmin performs two types of works—one which is performed at database level and other which is performed at the file system level. The users are required to provide all the inputs at the Adadmin prompt which normally involves choosing from the various options from the Adadmin menu. This doesn't mean that Adadmin can't be used non-interactively. You can run some task non-interactively also and this is really useful for scheduling routine tasks that require little or no user intervention.

5. Can adadmin be scheduled to run in a non-interactive mode?

Yes, adadmin can be scheduled to run at a later time in a non-interactive mode.

6. How is adadmin run in a non-interactive mode?

To run adadmin in non-interactive mode, you must at first create a defaults file. Once the defaults file is created, you can run the adadmin in non-interactive mode using this file. To create a defaults file, specify defaultsfile= <filename> at the Ad Administration command line. The defaults file must be located under APPL_TOP/admin/<SID>.

```
$ adadmin defaultsfile=APPL_TOP/admin/emstest
/default.txt
```

In order to choose which task the defaults file will run, you add *menu_option*= <menu choice> to the utility start command. For example,

```
adadmin
defaultsfile=$APPL_TOP/admin/emstest/
default.txt
logfile=adadmin.log
workers=10
interactive=no
menu_option=DISABLE_MAINT_MODE
```

The menu options for adadmin to be run in non-interactive mode are given below.

Menu option corresponding ad administration menu choice:

GEN_MESSAGES	Generate message files
GEN_FORMS	Generate form files
GEN_GRAPHICS	Generate graphics files
GEN_REPORTS	Generate reports files
GEN_JARS	Generate product JAR files
RELINK Relink	Applications programs
CREATE_ENV	Create Applications environment file
COPY_FILES	Copy files to destinations
CONVERT_CHARSET	Convert character set
SCAN_APPLTOP	Scan the APPL_TOP for exceptions
SCAM_CUSTOM_DIR	Scan a CUSTOM directory for exceptions
LIST_SNAPSHOT	List snapshots
UPDATE_CURRENT_VIEW	Update current view snapshot
CREATE_SNAPSHOT	Create named snapshot
EXPORT_SNAPSHOT	Export snapshot to file

(*Contd*)

IMPORT_SNAPSHOT	Import snapshot from file
DELETE_SNAPSHOT	Delete named snapshot
CHECK_FILES	Check for missing files
CMP_INVALID	Compile APPS schema
CMP_MENU	Compile menu information
CMP_FLEXFIELDS	Compile flexfield data in AOL tables
RELOAD_JARS	Reload JAR files to database
VALIDATE_APPS	Validate APPS schema
CREATE_GRANTS	Recreate grants and synonyms for APPS schema
MAINTAIN_MLS	Maintain multi-lingual tables
CHECK_DUAL	Check DUAL table
MAINTAIN_MRC	Maintain Multiple Reporting Currencies schema
CONVERT_MCURR	Convert to Multiple Reporting Currencies
CONVERT_MULTI_ORG	Convert to Multi-Org
ENABLE_MAINT_MODE	Enable Maintenance Mode
DISABLE_MAINT_MODE	Disable Maintenance Mode

7. What options are available in the adadmin main menu?

The following options are available in the adadmin main menu.

```
   AD Administration Main Menu
1. Generate Applications Files menu
2. Maintain Applications Files menu
3. Compile/Reload Applications Database
   Entities menu
4. Maintain Applications Database Entities
   menu
5. Change Maintenance Mode
6. Exit AD Administration
```

8. What are the adadmin activities that can be run in a parallel way?

The following adadmin tasks are supported to be run in parallel mode.

- Recreate grants and synonyms
- Compile APPS schema
- Maintain multiple reporting currencies schema
- Convert to Multi-org
- Generate message files
- Generate form files
- Generate report files

9. Which options of adadmin can and cannot be run in a non-interactive way?

Starting from AD.I all the options of the adadmin can be run in non-interactive way.

10. Do Ad utilities support the help option?

Yes, starting from AD.I all Ad utilities support the "help" option. The help can be invoked by typing

<AD Utility name> help=y

The only exception to this is admrgpch that takes -help option.

11. What does the option generate message files do in adadmin?

This is the first option in the menu of adadmin. This option takes care of generating all the Oracle message files. Oracle Application uses these files to display messages. This task generates message binary files (extension .msb) from Oracle Application library tables. Once this option is selected, it asks a couple of questions like the number of workers for parallel processing and the list of products for which the message files need to be generated.

12. How can you regenerate all the forms files using adadmin and what does it do internally?

The generate forms files option of adadmin takes care of generating the forms files (extension .fmx) from binary forms definition files (extension .fmb). These binary forms definition files are normally located at $AU_TOP, and the executables files are stored under each product's directory. Oracle Applications use the binary form files to display data entry forms. Like the previous option, this option also asks for a couple of questions before generating the forms. This task should be performed anytime you have issues with a form or a set of forms.

13. You have accidentally deleted the environment file. How can you recreate it?

You can recreate the environment file by using the option create applications file from adadmin. This option creates an environment file that defines your system configuration. It prompts for Oracle Applications environment name.

14. In adadmin there is an option validate APPS schema. What does it mean and what does it do?

Validating APPS schema means verifying the integrity of the APPS schema. It checks whether the apps schema has proper roles and privileges or not. It determines the problems you must fix specific to APPS schema as well as the problems you must fix not specific to the APPS schema. This task produces a report named <APPS schema name>.lst which is located at $APPL_TOP/admin/$TWO_TASK/out.

Validation of the APPS schema is in turn taken care by a SQL script advrfapp.sql. The location of the same is $AD_TOP/admin/sql. The same script can also be run from the sql prompt.

15. How do you recreate the grants and the synonyms for the APPS schema?

The recreation of the grants and the synonyms in the APPS schema can be done using the option recreate grants and synonym for the APPS schema available in the adadmin. This task takes care of recreating grants and synonyms for APPLSYSPUB, recreates grants on some packages from SYSTEM to APPS and recreating grants and synonyms for APPS schema.

Each product's data objects are created in its own schema (such as the GL schema) but the user accesses all data objects through the APPS schema, therefore the APPS schema must have the appropriate grants and synonyms for those objects.

This task runs two SQL files:

1. Runs $FND_TOP/admin/sql/afpub.sql to set up grants and synonyms for the Applications Public Schema (APPLSYSPUB by default)
2. Runs $AD_TOP/admin/sql/adappsgs.pls for every Oracle Applications base product schema

16. What is the significance of the DUAL table? Who owns this table and how many rows it should have?

The DUAL table is created automatically by Oracle along with the data dictionary. It is located in the schema of SYS. It has one column named DUMMY of type VARCHAR2 and contains one row with a value of 'X'. In case it has more than one row, application system may not function properly.

17. What is ad splice? What does it do?

Oracle often releases new products after the base release of Oracle Applications. These products are known as off cycle products. Ad splice is the utility which takes care of incorporating and off cycle product into Oracle Applications so that it is recognized by the ad utilities as a valid Oracle Application product. Ad splice registers off cycle products as active in the system and as a result the ad utilities recognize the off cycle products as valid product for a specific release. Then you can use adpatch to install the product's component file system and database object.

18. What does ad splice set up?

Ad splice sets up the following:

- the product's database account
- the product's physical location <PRODUCT>_TOP

- logical $<PRODUCT>_TOP—need to run the created environment file afterwards option

19. What are the three files which ad splice requires at the time of splicing?

The three files are newprods.txt, <prod>prod.txt and <prod>terr.txt, where <prod> refers to the product name.

20. Explain the significance of the ad splice control files.

Ad splice requires two types of control files.

- Product definition file: There are two product definition files per sliced product (prod_name)prod.txt which contains language independent information for product and (prod_name)terr.txt which contains language dependent information for the product. Since both of the files define the product and the associated language, these files must not be edited. The ad splice control files must be copied to the APPL_TOP/admin directory.
- Product configuration file: The product configuration newprods.txt file contains all the parameters which are required to splice a new product.

The following is the given entry from the newprods.txt

```
product=alr
base_product_top=*APPL_TOP*
oracle_schema=alr
sizing_factor=100
main_tspace=*Product_Name*D
index_tspace=*Product_Name*X
temp_tspace=*Temporary_Tablespace*
default_tspace=*Product_Name*D
```

The entries are discussed below.

- Product: This is the new product which will be spliced by ad splice. So this entry should not be edited.
- Base_product_top: This is the base directory which contains the new product which is normally the APPL_TOP.
- Oracle_schema: This identifies the Oracle schema where the database objects for this product are created. This should be the same as product name.
- Sizing factor: This is the sizing factor which the Oracle Applications use when creating the tables and index for this product. The default value of 100 refers to 100% which means that the objects are created with the defaults size as determined by Oracle and the default value is recommended.
- Main_tspace: This is the default tablespace for the product.
- Index_tspace: This is the default index tablespace for the product.
- Temp_tspace: This is the tablespace for the Oracle schema's temporary segments, for example, TEMP.
- Default_tspace: It specifies the default tablespace where this product's objects are created.

21. What is distributed AD?

Distributed AD is introduced after AD.H which allows workers processing to be distributed across multiple nodes. This can be used only on the application systems that are using a shared application tier file system. For example, to run an AutoPatch session with a total of nine workers, say four workers on the local node and five workers on a remote node, distributed AD can be used.

22. What is the advantage of distributed AD?

With distributed AD, the workers can utilize the additional resources of the remote nodes where they are running apart from the primary node. This capability improves scalability, performance, and resource utilization and completion of worker in a faster time.

23. What is maintaining snapshot information and how can it be done?

Basically, there are two types of snapshots: APPL_TOP snapshot and global snapshot. An APPL_TOP snapshot lists patches and versions of files in the APPL_TOP. A global snapshot lists patches and latest versions of files in the entire applications system (that is across all APPL_TOP). Both APPL_TOP snapshots and global snapshots may be either current view snapshots or named view snapshots. A current view snapshot is created once and updated to maintain a consistent view. A named view snapshot is a copy of the current view snapshot at a particular time (not necessarily the latest current view snapshot) and is not updated.

A complete current view snapshot is required for automatic prerequisite patch checking to operate. During the installation, RapidInstall created a current snapshot as a baseline. And, each time you run AutoPatch, it automatically creates a new (updated) snapshot so that the information is current as of the application of the patch.

The same can be done using the adadmin utility.

24. Which ad utility is used to restart the failed workers?

For restarting the failed workers the utility adctrl is used.

25. What is the hidden option in adctrl?

The eighth and last option in adctrl is the hidden option. It's used for skipping and restarting the failed workers.

26. Explain briefly the different status of the workers.

Following are the different status of workers:

Assigned	The manager assigned a job to the worker.
Completed	The worker completed the job.
Failed	The worker has encountered a problem and have failed.
Fixed, Restarted	You fixed the problem and the failed job has restarted.
Restarted	The worker has restarted a job.
Running	The worker is running a job.
Wait	The worker is idle.

27. Can adctrl be run in non-interactive way? If yes, how?

Yes, adctrl can be run in a non-interactive way exactly in the same way it runs for adadmin. The same defaults file which is used for the adadmin can also be used for running adctrl in non-interactive manner. Only the menu option needs to be added for running the adctrl in case same defaults file is used. If you want to create a new defaults file then the same can be created exactly in the same way as created for adadmin.

Given below is the example of running adcrtl in non-interactive mode:

```
adctrl interactive=n \
defaultsfile=$APPL_TOP/admin/emstest/
ctrldefs.txt \
menu_option=SHOW_STATUS \
logfile=adctrl.log
```

The menu option for the defaults file for adctrl is listed below:

ACKNOWLEDGE_QUIT	Tell manager that a worker acknowledges quit
INFORM_FAILURE	Tell manager that a worker failed its job
RESTART_JOB	Tell worker to restart a failed job
SHOW_STATUS	Show worker status
SHUTDOWN_WORKER	Tell worker to quit
START_WORKER	Restart a worker on the current machine

28. What is adrelink and why is it used?

Adrelink is the executable which is used to relink ad executables with Oracle product libraries contained within the Oracle Applications Technology Stack Oracle_Home. All product executables can be linked using the relink application executables menu on the adadmin maintain application files submenu except an ad executable which has to be manually relinked using ad relink. Normally programs that need to be updated after a patch are automatically relinked by AutoPatch.

29. What is the force=y option while using the adrelink.sh?

The option force=y will relink the executables regardless the status of the libraries or the object files. Force=n will relink only if the libraries or object files are more recent than the current executable program.

30. What is ODF comparison utility and how is it used?

The object description file comparison utility is known as adodfcmp. Each Oracle application product is made up of one or more building blocks. For example, Journal Entry is one building block of Oracle General Ledger. There is an object descriptor file (ODF) describing the tables, views, indexes, sequences and privilege sets for the particular building block.

The ODF comparison utility compares an ODF with the database objects in an Oracle account, detects any differences in database structure, and runs SQL statements to remove the differences, so that the objects in the account will match the descriptions in the ODF file. The ODF comparison utility is used to compare the data model of a customer's data to a standard set of data model files from the current Oracle application release. It can optionally modify the database to match the standard data model. ODF comparison compares the building block to the ODF.

7
Cloning

1. What is cloning and why is cloning of an instance required?

Cloning is the process of creating an identical copy of the Oracle application system. Cloning of application system is required due to the following reasons:

- creating a test copy of your production system before upgrading
- to test some patches
- periodically refreshing a test system from your production system in order to keep the test system up-to-date
- creating a development copy of your environment to be used by the developers
- moving an existing system to a different machine

2. How many types of cloning are available?

There are two types of cloning methods available for Oracle Applications. One is adclone and the other is rapidclone.

3. What is the difference between adclone and rapidclone?

Adclone is an Oracle provided utility to clone application system. This utility is used to clone application system for release

11.5.1 to 11.5.5 for systems which are not autoconfig enabled, whereas rapidclone is used for those systems which are autoconfig enabled.

4. What are the steps involved in adclone?

Adclone involves four simple steps:

- running rapid install
- copying the source database
- copying the source application file system
- updating the configuration information

5. What is rapidclone?

Rapidclone is the new cloning utility which is used for autoconfig enabled environments. Rapidclone leverages the new installation and configuration technology utilized by RapidInstall.

6. How do I determine if my application system is autoconfig enabled or not?

There are a couple of ways to check if the enviroment is autoconfig enabled or not. You can check your environment in the following ways:

- Open the environment file APPLSYS.env or APPSORA.env in your APPL_TOP. If the top of the file says that it is maintained by autoconfig, then your system is probably using autoconfig. Apart from those files, opening any other important configuration files gives the information this file is managed by autoconfig if your application system is maintained by autoconfig.
- Check for the applications context file in the APPL_TOP/ admin directory. This file will typically be named <SID>.xml

or <SID>_<HOSTNAME>.xml. If the application system is autoconfig enabled there will be a corresponding xml file

- Check for the applications context file in the RDBMS ORACLE_HOME under the appsutil directory. This file will typically be named <SID>.xml or <SID>_<HOSTNAME>.xml. If the application system is autoconfig enabled there will be a corresponding xml file

7. I have the context file in the APPL_TOP admin directory and all my configuration files also say that the application system is managed by autoconfig but when I login to the database server I am not able to see the context file. Is my application system really autoconfig enabled?

It means that autoconfig is not enabled in the database tier. You need to enable the autoconfig in the database tier also.

8. Can I clone an application system from one operating system to another?

Yes, you can do a cloning from one platform to another as long as the target application system platform is binary compatible with the source system platform. For example, you can do a cloning from a lower version of Solaris to higher version of Solaris but not from Solaris to Windows. Also within a same platform, you can clone from a 32bit source system to a 64bit target system.

9. My source and target platforms have different binaries. Say I have AIX platform in the source and I want the target platform in Linux. Is there any way I can clone the environment?

Yes, you can clone or migrate the application system from any platform to Linux or any supported Unix platform. For doing this, you need to refer the metalink note migrating to Linux within Oracle Applications.

10. Is it possible to clone from a single node installation to a multiple node installation?

Yes, you can clone a single node installation to a multiple node installation using the rapidclone.

11. Explain briefly the steps to clone from a single node to a multi-node cloning.

Once the database cloning is over, the next step is to login to the APPL_TOP as the owner of application file system viz, applmgr and run the adcfgclone.pl from the COMMON_TOP/clone bin. While running adcfgcolne.pl, it asks "Does the target system have more than one application tier server node". Enter yes. Then it prompts for the target system's concurrent processing node, admin node, forms node and the Web node. Fill in node details from where you want these processes to run. It then prompts for the various mount point details and creates the context file for you. Follow the same process from all the nodes.

12. You have a multi-node shared APPL_TOP. Explain briefly the cloning process for the same.

If you have a shared APPL_TOP then apart from running the adcfgcolne.pl you also need to run "adclonectx.pl sharedappltop" for sharing the APPL_TOP from all the nodes. In this case, you need to run adcfgclone.pl only from the first node and you can create the context file using the adclonectx.pl in the other nodes by giving the reference to the XML file of the first node. Then you need to run the txkSOHM.pl from $FND_TOP/patch/115/bin which will create the 8.0.6 and iAS Config Home for your application system.

13. Can you clone a multi-node APPL_TOP to a single node APPL_TOP? Explain briefly the process for the same.

Yes, you can clone a single node APPL_TOP from a multi-node APPL_TOP. For this, you have to merge multiple APPL_TOP and COMMON_TOP files system into a single APPL_TOP and COMMON_TOP. For doing the same, the first step would be to login to each application tier node and run the 'maintain snapshot task' from the adadmin. Once done, login to one of the APPL_TOP and run the adpreclone.pl for merging the APPL_TOP. The same can be run using the command:

$ cd <COMMON_TOP>/admin/scripts/<CONTEXT_NAME>

$ perl adpreclone.pl appsTier merge

Once done, you need to login to the other nodes and run the adpreclone.pl for merging all the APPL_TOP's but from the other nodes the command would be different.

Login as the APPLMGR user to each of the secondary nodes being merged and run:

$ cd <COMMON_TOP>/admin/scripts/<CONTEXT_NAME>

$ perl adpreclone.pl appltop merge

For creating a clone of the multi-node APPL_TOP to a single node APPL_TOP you need to merge all the multi-node APPL_TOPs to a single APPL_TOP. You can merge all the APPL_TOPs together in a separate mount point so that the source application system is not affected with the clone.

Copy the following directories from first node to the place you want to create the merged APPL_TOP.

<APPL_TOP>

<OA_HTML> (when this directory exists)

<OA_JAVA>

<COMMON_TOP>/util

<COMMON_TOP>/clone

<COMMON_TOP>/_pages (when this directory exists)

<806 ORACLE_HOME>

<iAS ORACLE_HOME>

From the other APPL_TOPs recursively copy:

directory <COMMON_TOP>/clone/appl

- to -

directory <COMMMON_TOP>/clone/appl on the merged APPL_TOP

Configure the merged APPL_TOP by running the command

$ cd <COMMON_TOP>/clone/bin

$ perl adcfgclone.pl appsTier

It will create the single node APPL_TOP in the regular way.

14. Does rapid cloning take care of updating all the profile options?

Rapidclone only takes care of the site level profile options. All the other profile options need to be manually updated.

15. How do you prepare the template before cloning the application system?

You can prepare the template executing the following commands from the database and the application tier.

- At database tier: Login as Oracle user and run the following
  cd <RDBMS ORACLE_HOME>/appsutil/scripts/<CONTEXT_NAME>

  perl adpreclone.pl dbTier
- At the Application tier: Login as applmgr and run the following:

  cd <COMMON_TOP>/admin/scripts/<CONTEXT_NAME>perl adpreclone.pl appsTier

16. From the APPL_TOP, what are the files that you need to copy for creating a clone application system?

You need to copy the following files from the APPL_TOP

- APPL_TOP
- OA_HTML
- OA_JAVA
- OA_JRE_TOP
- COMMON_TOP>/util
- COMMON_TOP>/clone
- COMMON_TOP>/_pages (if this directory exists)
- 806 ORACLE_HOME
- iAS ORACLE_HOME

17. What exactly happens when you run adpreclone.pl? Does it anyway effect the source application system?

adpreclone.pl prepares the source system to be cloned by collecting information about the database and creates various templates of files containing source specific hardcoded values. It collects all the information about the source application system, the port numbers of the source application system etc. These templates are stored in the appsutil/template directory.

18. If you are told to clone a environment manually without using rapidclone, how will you do it?

For doing a manual clone, you need to change all the configuration files with the correct path of the APPL_TOP, product top, database SID, and port numbers. For doing the same, you need to change the following important configuration files.

$APPL_TOP/APPLSYS.env or APPSORA.env

$APPL_TOP/admin/adovars.env

$APPL_TOP/admin/hostname_twotask.xml

$APPL_TOP/admin/topfile.txt

$APPL_TOP/admin/adjborg.txt

$APPL_TOP/admin/adjborg2.txt

$FND_TOP/secure/hostname_twotask.dbc

$OA_HTML/bin/appsweb.cfg

Once these changes are done, you need to update the FND_PROFILE_OPTIONS value table in the database with the correct values of all the profiles and the FND_NODES with the node information. Here we are assuming that you are keeping the existing technology stack for doing the cloning. If you are bringing the technology stack also from the source env, you also need to change all the apache configuration files with the correct port and then need to link the iAS_ORACLE_HOME and the middle tier ORACLE_HOME and then run the autoconfig. Once done, start all the services.

19. How can you reduce time in cloning? What are the steps you can follow to clone an environment quickly?

These are the steps you can follow to clone an env quickly. If the technology stack of the source and the target environemnt are at the same patch level then you need not copy the 8.0.6 ORACLE_HOME and the IAS_ORACLE_HOME everytime. You can keep the existing technology stack. Before deleting the APPL_TOP, you can take a backup of the existing context file (the xml file in $APPL_TOP/admin) and then once the APPL_TOP and COMMON_TOP copy is done then you can revert back the same xml file rather than regenerating the same. If you are using the same XML file, you need not run the rapidclone as simply running of autoconfig will take care of all the things. In case you are using the shared APPL_TOP, you need to run the script txtSOHM.pl from $FND_TOP/patch/115/bin which will create the 8.0.6 and iAS Config Home for your application system.

20. Can I clone a cloned application system?

Yes, you can clone a cloned application system.

21. Is it possible that I use different set of ports for the cloned application system rather than the one which I am using for the source application system?

Yes, you can choose any port pool for the cloned application system. Adclone prompts for the port pool at that time put the port pool in which you want to run the application system.

22. How adcfgclone.pl knows the values for the target application system?

adcfgclone.pl prompts for the values required to create the new context file used to configure the target system. You need to provide the values for the prompts which adcfgclone.pl uses for creating and configuring the target application system.

23. What are the various questions that adcfgclone.pl prompts for and what should I answer to the prompts?

In the database tier, it prompts for the following:

- Target database SID
- Target system domain name
- Target instance is a Real Application Cluster (RAC) instance (y/n)
- Current node is the first node in an N Node RAC Cluster (y/n)

The tool will then ask for the number of nodes that will exist in the final RAC instance and gather, the following information for every node:

- Hostname
- Database Sid
- Instance number
- Listener port
- Private interconnect name
- RDBMS ORACLE_HOME path
- Number of DATA_TOP
- DATA_TOP mount points

In the application tier, it prompts for the following:

- Database server hostname
- Does the target system have more than one application tier server node (y/n)

The tool with them prompt for the hostnames of:

- concurrent processing node
- administration node
- forms server node
- Web server node
- Is the target system APPL_TOP divided into multiple mount points (y/n)?

If yes, the tool will then prompt for each auxiliary mount information.

- APPL_TOP mount point
- APPL_TOP aux.1
- APPL_TOP aux.2
- APPL_TOP aux.3
- COMMON_TOP mount point
- 8.0.6 ORACLE_HOME mount point
- iAS ORACLE_HOME mount point
- Location of JDK 1.3.1
- Port pool number:[0–99]

24. Does clone preserve the patch history?

Yes, Rapid Clone preserves the patch history. The following patch history is preserved even after the clone.

- RDBMS ORACLE_HOME: preserve the OUI oraInventory.
- iAS ORACLE_HOME: preserve the OUI oraInventory.
- 806 ORACLE_HOME: preserve the patch level and Oracle inventory.
- APPL_TOP and Database: preserve the patch level and history tables.

8
Upgradation

1. Is the upgrade process same if you want to upgrade to 11.5.10 from 11i and non-11i instances?

No, the upgrade process is different if you are upgrading from an 11i instance to 11.5.10 and from non-11i instance to 11.5.10.

2. What are the pre-upgrade steps that need to be taken for the upgradation of a non-11i instance to 11.5.10?

The important steps that need to be taken before an upgrade are:

- You need to take a complete backup of the application system
- You need to run the TUMS utility
- You need to review the TUMS report
- You need to maintain the multilingual tables
- You need to rename the custom database objects
- You need to check attachment file upload directory
- You need to save the custom.pll

3. What is TUMS? Why is it required to run TUMS before doing an upgrade?

TUMS is a utility to help customers reduce the number of steps necessary in the upgrade. It looks at a customer's specific situation, and identifies which steps are irrelevant for that customer. The output of TUMS can be used to reduce upgrade time. The upgrade manual script (TUMS) is used to create a report that lists the upgrade steps that don't apply to Oracle Application installation. You can ignore the steps that are generated with the report of TUMS.

For generating the TUMS report, you need to download and apply the TUMS 3422686 patch from metalink using the adpatch utility. The TUMS patch needs to be applied for both 10.7 and 11.0.x version of Oracle Applications.

Once the patch is applied successfully, the adtums.sql script is used to generate the TUMS report. For the <DIRECTORY> value, enter the full path of the directory that you want the TUMS report to be written to. This directory must be listed in the UTL_FILE_DIR parameter of your init.ora before TUMS can write the report and must have the appropriate permissions to write the report (tums.html).

4. After the application of the TUMS patch, where does the script adtums.sql need to be run from?

If you are upgrading from release 10.7, the script needs to be run from the following location:

For UNIX users:

```
$ cd $AD_TOP/patches/107/sql
$ sqlplus <APPS username>/<APPS password>
@adtums.sql <DIRECTORY>
```

For Windows users:

```
C:\> cd %AD_TOP%\patches\107\sql
C:\> sqlplus <APPS username>/<APPS password>
@adtums.sql <DIRECTORY>
```

If you are upgrading from release 11.0, the script needs to be run from the following location:

For UNIX users:

```
$ cd $AD_TOP/patch/110/sql
$ sqlplus <APPS username>/<APPS password>
@adtums.sql <DIRECTORY>
```

For Windows users:

```
C:\> cd %AD_TOP%\patch\110\sql
C:\> sqlplus <APPS username>/<APPS password>
@adtums.sql <DIRECTORY>
```

5. What is the significance of custom.pll and what does it contain?

Custom.pll is the custom library. If you have done some customizations in Oracle Applications, you must preserve the custom library (custom.pll) which contains the details of the customizations done in the application system. It is used to migrate to 11i.

6. What is the actual upgrade process for doing an upgrade for a non-11i application system?

Once all the pre-upgrade tasks are done, we can start the actual upgrade. The upgrade starts with running RapidInstall. It needs to run twice—one for doing the actual upgrade and secondly, for configuring all application systems once the upgrade is complete. This is the sequence in which the upgrade works from a 10.7 or 11.0.x release to 11.5.10CU2.

- Enter configuration parameters and run RapidInstall
- Run autoUpgrade to upgrade products and database objects
- Run AutoPatch to apply the patches
- Run RapidInstall to configure and start all the servers and services

7. If I run the RapidInstall, does it mean that it creates a new application system for me? What happens to the existing database?

RapidInstall connects to the existing database and creates the new database ORACLE_HOME, APPL_TOP and the Tech stack. Once the RapidInstall is run, you need to migrate the existing database to 9i run AutoUpgrade and then to switch to the new application system. Once this is done, you need to take care of all the customizations in the new APPL_TOP, apply the required patches and then run the RapidInstall again to configure all the servers.

8. What is AutoUpgrade and why do we need to run AutoUpgrade?

Once the RapidInstall is run successfully the next step is to run AutoUpgrade. It is used to upgrade Oracle applications product from the earlier version to the base version of the latest release. It can be started from the command prompt by invoking the AutoUpgrade utility by typing adaimgr.

9. Where is the location of the adaimgr log files?

1. If the environment variable $APPLCSF is set, the default location is $APPLCSF/$APPLLOG
2. If the environment variable $APPLCSF is not set, the logs go to $FND_TOP/$APPLLOG

10. Explain briefly the steps in the AutoUpgrade process.

There are three steps in the AutoUpgrade process:

1. *Choosing database parameters*

The first option is the adaimgr main menu which is used for choosing the database parameters. From this screen, you can do the following:

- Changing the default Oracle user id and password for each product
- Setting the sizing factor for new objects of a product or for new products
- Setting the tablespaces for new products
- Changing the tablespaces for existing product

2. *Choosing overall tasks and their parameters*

   This is the second option in the AutoUpgrade main menu. It displays the tasks that AutoUpgrade will do during the upgrade processing. You can do the following from this screen.

   - Create applications environment file
   - Verify files necessary for install/upgrade
   - Install or upgrade database objects

3. *Running the selected tasks*

   This is the third step in the AutoUpgrade process. Here it prompts for the following:

   - How do you wish to enable parallel concurrent processing
   - Do you wish to use the 8.3 file name convention [No]
   - Enter the common area for the log and the out files
   - Enter the directory for applications temporary files
   - Enter the directory for reports temporary files
   - Enter the Web server host machine
   - Enter the port number

   Once all the information is given, the AutoUpgrade starts running and verifies the files for all the products one by one.

11. Explain in detail what are the pre-upgrade steps for upgrading to 11.5.10 for 11i application system?

The following are the pre-upgrade steps for upgrade process for 11i application system.

Announcing downtime

The first step towards an upgrade is announcing a downtime. All the users must be communicated with the downtime well in advance and the downtime should be planned in such a way that it affects the least in terms of revenue. Ideally the upgrade should be planned in weekends or holidays where you can afford to have a downtime.

Backing up application system

A full backup of the database and the APPL_TOP must be taken before starting the upgrade process so that in case of any upgrade failures you can revert back to the existing system. A cold backup of the database should be taken with the normal shutdown.

Running TUMS utility

TUMS is a utility to help customers reduce the number of steps necessary in the upgrade. It looks at a customer's specific situation, and identifies which steps are irrelevant for that customer. The output of TUMS can be used to reduce upgrade time. The upgrade manual script (TUMS) is used to create a report that lists the upgrade steps that don't apply to Oracle Application installation. You can ignore the steps that are generated with the report of TUMS.

The TUMS for 11.5.10 maintenance pack report will be created in the directory UTL_FILE_DIR. So make sure that this directory has proper write permission.

Once the patch is applied successfully, the TUMS report can be generated using the following command:

```
$ cd $AD_TOP/patch/115/sql
$ sqlplus <APPS username>/<APPS password>
@adtums.sql <DIRECTORY>
```

For updating the auto config tech stack components, you need to apply the patch 4489303. Make sure you follow all the steps as mentioned in the readme of the patch.

Running tech stack validation utility

Apply the patch 4318672 in all the nodes of the APPL_TOP to install the utility which verifies the minimum technology stack components version and the other configuration requirements which are associated with the 11.5.10 CU 2 maintenance pack. Once this patch is applied you need to run the technology stack validation utility at the APPL_TOP as well as at the database. The utility can be run with the following command:

At APPL_TOP

```
$ADPERLPRG $FND_TOP/patch/115/bin/TXKScript.pl
 -script=$FND_TOP/patch/115/bin/
   txkVal11510MP.pl
 -txktop=$APPLTMP
 -appspass=<apps_password>
 -outfile=$APPLTMP/txkVal11510MP.html
```

At Database

```
$ADPERLPRG  $ORACLE_HOME/appsutil/bin/
TXKScript.pl
 -script=$ORACLE_HOME/appsutil/bin/
   txkVal11510MP.pl
 -txktop=$ORACLE_HOME/appsutil
 -appspass=<apps_password>
 -outfile=$ORACLE_HOME/appsutil/temp/
   txkVal11510MP_DB.html
```

The utility must return the "[ALLPASS]" status on each application tier server node as well as database server nodes in order for you to be able to continue with the installation of the release 11.5.10 maintenance pack. If the "[FAIL]" status is returned for any test on any node, you must take the specified action to fix the problem, re-run the utility on each node that reported a failure, and ensure that the "[ALLPASS]" status is returned.

Converting to OATM model (Optional)

The 11.5.10 release of Oracle Application introduces a new Oracle Application Tablespace Model (OATM) consisting only twelve tablespaces. In this model, each database object is mapped to a tablespace based on its input output characteristics, which include object size, life span, access methods and locking granularity. This model facilitates easier maintenance, reduced space usage, and run-time performance gains for Oracle applications. The OATM uses locally managed tablespaces. In previous release of 11i, each product was allocated two separate tablespaces—one for index and the other for data. But with OATM the total number of tablespace has been reduced to 12 including temporary tablespace, system tablespace, and undo segments. If your application system is on a previous release then you can switch to OATM model using the Oracle Application Tablespace Migration Utility. This is an optional step.

Configuring database for new products

The database must be configured for the new products, which are added since the release of 11i. For this, you need to apply the patch 3180164 which takes care of adding the new product details in your environment. Follow all the steps as mentioned in the readme of the patch.

Product specific steps

Apart from these steps there are many product specific pre-install steps that need to be done before the application of the maintenance pack. Since these tasks are specifically related to products that are installed so we are not discussing the same here. You must check this with the Oracle manual while doing an upgrade.

12. Explain in details the actual upgrade steps for upgrading to 11.5.10 for an 11i application system.

The following are the actual upgrade steps for upgrading to 11.5.10 for an 11i application system.

Stop middle tiers

Shutdown all the components of the middle tiers before starting the patching. For stopping the same, you can use the script adstpall.sh which is located in the $APPLCSF/scripts/<sid> directory.

Upgrading database

Before applying the 11.5.10 CU2, the database must be upgraded to 9i release 2 or a higher version of Oracle RDBMS. If you are planning to upgrade to 9.2.0 version then you must follow the steps given in the metalink note 216550.1 and if you are planning to upgrade to 10g release 1 then you must follow the steps given in the metalink note 282038.1.

Apply 11.5.10 CU 2 maintenance pack

Apply the 11.5.10 CU 2 patch 3480000. In case you have a multiple node APPL_TOP then the patch should be applied at the admin tier at first and then should be applied in all the other nodes of the APPL_TOP one by one. If you have any other languages installed other than American English then you must apply the NLS patch immediately after the base patch. In case you are upgrading from release 11.5.4 or earlier version, you must run the adadmin and choose the option "Maintain multi-lingual tables". The NLS patch also needs to be applied from all the nodes in case of a multiple node installation.

The autopatch also takes care of performing the post-installation steps during the patching itself like compiling Apps schema, compiling the flexfields, maintaining MRC, compiling JSPs, generating JAR files, generating forms etc. which earlier needs to be done manually after patching.

13. What are the post-upgrade steps that need to be followed once the upgrade is done?

The following are the post-upgrade steps.

Start middle tiers

Once the 11.5.10 CU 2 patch has been successfully applied, you can start all the middle tiers. You are starting the middle tiers for testing purpose only, so the access to the users to the application system should not be given till you complete all the steps.

Registering new products

The new products, that are added, don't get registered in the database automatically. They need to be done manually. For this, you have to use the license manager which can be invoked using the Oracle Applications Manager.

Dropping MRC schema

The Multiple Reporting Currencies (MRC) schema is no longer used anymore. You can safely drop the schema at any time. This can be done online also and no downtime is required for this. The following script needs to run for doing the same.

```
$ cd $APPL_TOP/admin
$ sqlplus SYSTEM/<SYSTEM password>
@addrpmrc.sql <APPLSYS_USERNAME> SAFE
```

Product-specific tasks

Apart from all these tasks, there are a lot many product-specific tasks that need to be done as a part of Oracle Application Upgradation. Consult the Oracle manual for getting a list of all those tasks.

Sanity testing

Once all the product specific tasks are done, do a sanity test to check that the environment is working fine. If you are facing some issue after the upgradation, then contact the Oracle support with full details of the error.

Announce environment to users

Once the sanity testing is done and all the logins are working fine then announce the environment to the users so that they can start using it. Take a complete backup of the environment as soon as possible.

14. How can you upgrade the database or the techstack using the RapidInstall?

For starting the database or techstack upgrade using the RapidInstall, the RapidInstall screen is invoked by typing rapidwiz – techstack from the command prompt. It then gives two options to choose from

Upgrading to 9i ORACLE_HOME

Upgrading to 9iAS 1.0.2.2.2.

9
R12

1. What are the important technological changes in the Release 12?

The important change in the technological stack is that the 8.0.6 ORACLE_HOME and the IAS_ORACLE_HOME have been replaced by Oracle Application Server 10g 10.1.2 and Oracle Application Server 10g 10.1.3, respectively.

The technology stack of the application tier consists of the following components.

Oracle Developer 10i, which includes

- Oracle Forms
- Oracle Reports

Oracle Application Server 10g 10.1.2 (formerly known as 8.0.6 ORACLE_HOME)

Oracle Application Server 10g 10.1.3 (includes Oracle HTTP Server, formerly known as iAS_ORACLE_HOME)

2. What are the changes in the desktop tier in R12?

In the desktop tier, the new Sun J2SE plug-in replaces the traditional Oracle JInitiator which was used till the 11i release. The J2SE plug-in is automatically downloaded and installed when the Forms-based applications are called. For example, if you select the System Administrator responsibility and click the responsibility Security > User > Define, you will get a message like this for the installation of the J2SE.

In order to access this application, you must install the J2SE plug-in version 1.5.0_07. To install this plug-in, click here to download the oaj2se.exe executable. Once the download is complete, double-click the oaj2se.exe file to install the plug-in. You will be prompted to restart your browser when the installation is complete.

Once you download and install the plug-in, you will be able to run Forms-based applications.

The Forms client applet and commonly used JAR files are downloaded from the Web server at the beginning of the client's first session. Less commonly used JAR files are downloaded as needed. All downloaded JAR files are cached locally on the client, ready for future sessions.

In R12, the cache directory path is of the form:

<HOMEDRIVE>\Documents and Settings\<Windows User Name>\Application Data\Sun\Java\Deployment\cache

For example:

C:\Documents and Settings\jobanerj\Application Data\Sun\Java\Deployment\cache

3. What are the components of the Application Server 10.1.3 (formerly known as IAS_ORACLE_HOME)?

- Oracle Containers for Java (OC4J)
- Oracle Process Manager and Notification Server (OPMN)
- Oracle HTTP Server (OHS) 10.1.3.0.0 (Apache 1.3.34)

4. What is OC4J?

The Jserv is replaced by OC4J. This is included in the 10.1.3 ORACLE_HOME. OC4J runs on the Java virtual machine and is based on Java 2 Enterprise Edition (J2EE) standards. You can have multiple OC4J processes running, each of which is referred to as an OC4J instance. The OC4J configuration is controlled via XML configuration files and OC4J properties file. An OC4J instance is referred to as a container as it provides a Web container to support services like Java Server Pages (JSP), Servlets, Enterprise Java Beans (EJB) and Web Services.

5. How many instances of OC4J are created in R12?

The R12 creates 3 OC4J instances:

- Oacore (runs OA Framework-based applications),
- Forms (runs Forms-base applications),
- OAFM (runs the Web services, mapviewer, application server control)

6. What is OPMN and what are its components?

Oracle Process Manager is the centralized process management mechanism in Oracle Application Server and is used to manage Oracle Application Server processes. The Process Manager is responsible for starting, restarting, stopping and monitoring every process it manages. The Process Manager handles all requests sent to OPMN associated with controlling a process or obtaining status about a process. The Process Manager is also responsible for performing death-detection and automatic restart of the processes it manages. OPMN manages AS components and consists of:

- Oracle Notification Server (ONS). It is the transport mechanism for failure, recovery, startup and other related notifications between components in Oracle Application Server. It operates according to a publish-subscribe model. An Oracle Application Server component receives a notification of a certain type for each subscription to ONS.

When such a notification is published, ONS sends it to the appropriate subscribers.

- Delivers notifications between components OHS <->OPMN<->OC4J

7. **Explain briefly the major changes in the file system in R12.**

There are lots of changes in the file system in the new R12. The new structure splits the Oracle Application files in three parts.

- Data
- Code
- Config

Separating these three helps in easy maintenance as configuration file changes more frequently than the code and the data.

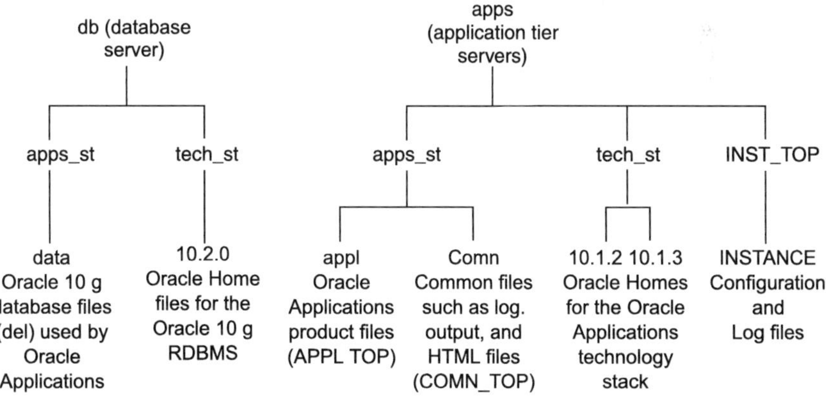

- The db/apps_st/data (DATA_TOP) directory contains all the data files, redo log file and is located on the database node.
- The db/tech_st/10.2.0 contains the ORACLE_HOME for the Oracle10g database and is located in the database node.

- The apps/apps_st/appl (APPL_TOP) directory contains the product directories and files for Oracle Applications.
- The apps/apps_st/comn or (COMMON_TOP or COMN_TOP) directory contains the common directories and files used across products.
- The apps/tech_st/10.1.2 directory contains the ORACLE_HOME used for the Applications technology stack tools components.
- The apps/tech_st/10.1.3directory contains the ORACLE_HOME used for the applications technology stack Java components.
- The INST_TOP contains all the configuration files and log files.

8. **What is Instance Top? What are the advantages of Instance Top?**

   R12 introduces a new concept of a top-level directory for an Applications Instance which is known as Instance Home and is denoted the environment variable $INST_TOP. Instance Home contains all the config files, log files, ssl certificates, etc. The addition Instance Home makes the middle tier easier to manage and organize since the data is kept separated from the config files. It also has the ability to share the Applications and Technology stack code across multiple instances. To create a new instance that shares an existing middle-tier, create a new instance_top with proper config files and nfs mount the middle tier in the server.

   Another advantage of the Instance Home is that the Autoconfig no longer writes anything to the APPL_TOP and ORACLE_HOME directories. Everything is now written in the INST_TOP and as a result APPL_TOP and ORACLE_HOME can also be made read only file system if required. Earlier the adpatch used to write the log file in

APPL_TOP/admin directory but with the new model the APPL_CONFIG_HOME/admin is used.

The basic structure of the Instance Home is:

<APPS_BASE>/inst/apps/<context>/<INST_TOP>, where APPS_BASE (which does not have or need a corresponding environment variable) is the top level of the Applications installation, and <context> is the highest level at which the Applications context exists.

9. What is the directory structure of an Instance Top?

Given below is the directory structure for the Instance Top.

$INST_TOP

/admin	
/scripts	ADMIN_SCRIPTS_HOME: Find all AD scripts here
/appl	APPL_CONFIG_HOME. For standalone envs, this is set to $APPL_TOP
/fnd/12.0.0/secure	FND_SECURE: dbc files here
/admin	All Env Config files here
/certs	SSL Certificates go here
/logs	LOG_HOME: Central log file location. All log files are placed here (except adconfig)
/ora	ORA_CONFIG_HOME
/10.1.2	'C' Oracle home config, Contains tnsnames and forms listener servlet config files
/10.1.3	Apache and OC4J config home, Apache, OC4J and opmn. This is the 'Java'

	Oracle home configuration for OPMN, Apache and OC4J
/pids	Apache/Forms server PID files here
/portal	Apache's DocumentRoot folder

10. Explain the difference in the mount points between 11i and R12.

The differences are given in the below mentioned table.

	For Applmgr User	
Mount Point	**11i**	**R12**
APPL_TOP	<APPS_BASE>/<SID>appl	<APPS_BASE>/apps/apps_st/appl
COMMON_TOP	<APPS_BASE>/<SID>comn	<APPS_BASE>/apps/apps_st/comn
ORACLE_HOME	<APPS_BASE>/<SID>ora/8.0.6	<APPS_BASE>/apps/tech_st/10.1.2
IAS_ORACLE_HOME	<APPS_BASE>/<SID>ora/iAS	<APPS_BASE>/apps/tech_st/10.1.3
	For Oracle User	
Mount Point	**11i**	**R12**
ORACLE_HOME	<ORACLE_BASE>/<SID>db/10.2.0	<ORACLE_BASE>/db/tech_st/10.2.0
ORADATA	<ORACLE_BASE>/<SID>data	<ORACLE_BASE>/db/apps_st/data
	INSTANCE_HOME	
Mount Point	**11i**	**R12**
INST_TOP	NA	<APPS_BASE>/inst/apps/<context_name>

11. What is the default mode of forms service in R12?

In R12, by default the forms service are provided by forms servlet mode.

12. What are the advantages of forms servlet mode?

Following are the advantages of running forms in servlet mode.

- The dropped network connection can be re-established.
- Firewall/proxy server is easy to configure.
- Only a few machines and ports needs to be exposed at firewall.
- It's a very secured protocol in the Internet.

13. What happened to the Reports server in R12?

The Reports server is obsolete in R12. All reports are now run through the Concurrent Processing server manager via the rwrun executable, which spawns an in-process server.

14. How is the directory structure of COMMON_TOP in R12?

The directory structure of the COMMON_TOP in R12 is shown in the diagram given below.

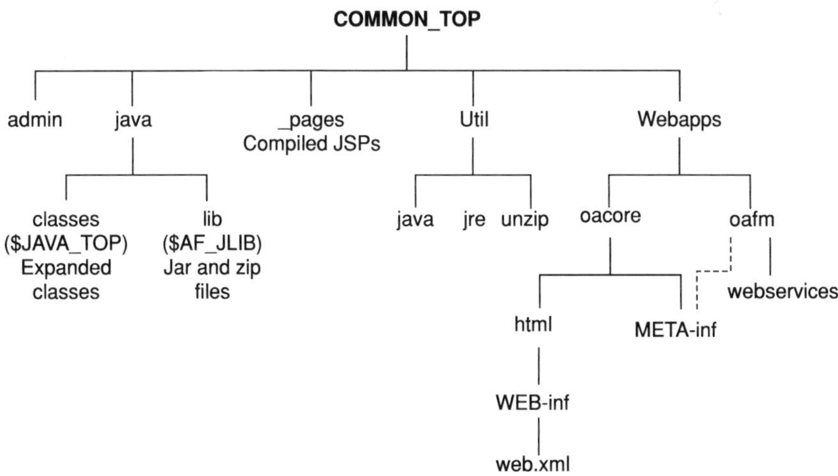

15. What are the important xml configuration files that are introduced in R12?

The XML configuration files are:

- opmn.xml
- server.xml
- orion-application.xml
- orion-web.xml

16. What is OPMN.XML used for? What is the location of this file?

OPML.xml is used by OPMN. It contains details of all the OC4J instances deployed on the server. This file is located at $ORA_CONFIG_HOME/10.1.3/opmn/conf/.

17. What is SERVER.XML used for? What is the location of this file?

This file is used by OC4J. It contains details of all the applications deployed under that OC4J instance like name of the application, where it is deployed, shared libraries if any. This is located at $ORA_CONFIG_HOME/10.1.3/j2ee/oacore/config/.

18. What is ORION-APPLICATION.XML used for? What is the location of this file?

This file is used by application instance. It contains details of all the Web modules deployed under that application. It also includes library path where it should look for the Java code. This is located at $ORA_CONFIG_HOME/10.1.3/j2ee/oacore/applications-deployment/oacore.

19. What is ORION-WEB.XML used for? What is the location of this file?

This file is used by Web module. It contains details of all servlet aliases and the mapping to servlet classes. This is located at

$ORA_CONFIG_HOME/10.1.3/j2ee/oacore/applications-deployment/oacore/html/.

20. What are the important forms configuration files in R12 and where are they located?

The forms configuration files are located at $ORA_CONFIG_HOME/10.1.2/forms/server. The forms configuration files are:

- appsweb.cfg ($FORMS_WEB_CONFIG_FILE). This file has moved to this location. It contains info on serverName, serverPort etc.
- default.env. It contains most of the env variables (classpath, product tops, oracle home etc.).

21. What are the various log file locations in R12?

The various log file locations are given below. In R12, all the log files are located at Instance Top.

• AD Script log files	$INST_TOP/logs/appl/admin/log
• CM log files	$INST_TOP/logs/appl/conc/log
• AD tools log files	$APPL_CONFIG_HOME/admin/$TWO_TASK/log
• OPMN log files	$INST_TOP/logs/10.1.3/opmn
• Apache log files	$INST_TOP/logs/10.1.3/Apache/
• OC4J log files (Text)	$INST_TOP/logs/10.1.3/j2ee/oacore/
• OC4J log files	$INST_TOP/logs/10.1.3/j2ee/oacore/log/oacore_default_group_1/oc4j

22. What is the location of the DBC file in R12?

The DBC file is located at $INST_TOP/appl/fnd/12.0.0/secure/<SID>.dbc

23. What is the location of the RapidInstallation logs in R12?

The RapidInstall logs are given below.

Before the Installations

$TMP/<MMDDHHMM>/<MMDDHHMM>.log
$TMP/<MMDDHHMM>/<hostname>_<SID>.xml
$TMP/<MMDDHHMM>/<hostname>_<SID>_apps.xml

The Rapidwiz Configuration File is saved in 3 locations.

$TMP/<MMDDHHMM>/conf_<SID>.txt

$INST_TOP/conf_<SID>.txt

<RDBMS ORACLE_HOME>/appsutil/conf_<SID>.txt

Database Tier

$ORACLE_HOME/appsutil/log/$CONTEXT_NAME/<MMDDHHMM>.log $ORACLE_HOME/appsutil/log/$CONTEXT_NAME/ApplyDBTechStack_<MMDDHHMM>.log

$ORACLE_HOME/appsutil/log/$CONTEXT_NAME/ohclone.log

$ORACLE_HOME/appsutil/log/$CONTEXT_NAME/make_<MMDDHHMM>.log

$ORACLE_HOME/appsutil/log/$CONTEXT_NAME/installdbf.log

$ORACLE_HOME/appsutil/log/$CONTEXT_NAME/adcrdb_<SID>.log $ORACLE_HOME/appsutil/log/$CONTEXT_NAME/ApplyDatabase_<MMDDHHMM>.log

$ORACLE_HOME/appsutil/log/$CONTEXT_NAME/<MMDDHHMM>/adconfig.log
$ORACLE_HOME/appsutil/log/$CONTEXT_NAME/<MMDDHHMM>/NetServiceHandler.log

Applications Tier(s)

$INST_TOP/logs/<MMDDHHMM>.log

$APPL_TOP/admin/$CONTEXT_NAME/log/ApplyAppsTechStack.log

$INST_TOP/logs/ora/10.1.2/install/make_<MMDDHHMM>.log

$INST_TOP/logs/ora/10.1.3/install/make_<MMDDHHMM>.log

$INST_TOP/admin/log/ApplyAppsTechStack.log

$INST_TOP/admin/log/ohclone.log

$APPL_TOP/admin/$CONTEXT_NAME/log/installAppl.log

$APPL_TOP/admin/$CONTEXT_NAME/log/ApplyAppltop_<MMDDHHMM>.log

$APPL_TOP/admin/$CONTEXT_NAME/log/<MMDDHHMM>/adconfig.log $APPL_TOP/admin/$CONTEXT_NAME/log/<MMDDHHMM>/NetServiceHandler.log

Inventory Registration

<Global Inventory>/logs/cloneActions<timestamp>.log
<Global Inventory>/logs/oraInstall<timestamp>.log
<Global Inventory>/logs/silentInstall<timestamp>.log

24. R12 introduces the concept of "Service Groups". What exactly are service groups?

A server is the traditional term for a process that provides a particular functionality. This term, in the sense of a denoting a single process, is less appropriate for the R12 architecture, so the replacement term of service is used where applicable. Related services make up service groups.

25. What are the various service groups in R12 and what are the services they support?

Service Groups	*Supports*
Root Service Group	• Oracle Process Manager (OPMN)
Web Entry Point Services	• HTTP Server
Web Application Services	• OACORE OC4J • Forms OC4J • OAFM OC4J
Batch Processing Services	• Applications TNS Listener • Concurrent Managers • Fulfillment Server
Other Service Group	• Oracle Forms Services • Oracle MWA Service

26. How are these service groups related with Web, Forms and Concurrent Processing tier? How do I know which service group should be enabled in which tier?

Applications nodes should have services enabled as follows:

• Web node	Root Service Group, Web Entry Point Services, Web Application Services
• Forms node	Root Service Group, Web Application Services, Other Service Group
• Concurrent Processing node	Root Service Group, Batch Processing Services

27. Can you give an example to illustrate which service group should be enabled in which tier? Also what happens to the various ORACLE_HOMEs?

Let's assume that we want to do a two-node installation in two linux boxes say, LinuxServer1 and LinuxServer2 and want to install the database and the concurrent processing in LinuxServer1 and the Web and Forms Services in the LinuxServer2 then

- On LinuxServer1, you would select Root Service Group and Batch ProcessingServices.
- On LinuxServer2, you would select Root Service Group, Web Entry Point Services, Web Application Services, and Other Service Group.

In terms of ORACLE_HOME creation, the result will be that:

- LinuxServer1 will have an ORACLE_HOME for the 10g R2 Applications database, plus an ORACLE_HOME for Application Server 10.1.2, and an ORACLE_HOME for Application Server 10.1.3.
- LinuxServer2 will have an ORACLE_HOME for Application Server 10.1.2, and an ORACLE_HOME for Application Server 10.1.3.

28. What are the various scripts available in R12? What are their locations?

The scripts are located at $INST_TOP/admin/scripts.

- adautocfg.sh run autoconfig
- adstpall.sh stop all services
- adstrtal.sh start all services
- adapcctl.sh start/stop/status Apache only
- adformsctl.sh start/stop/status OC4J Forms
- adoacorectl.sh start/stop/status OC4J oacore
- adopmnctl.sh start/stop/status opmn
- adalnctl.sh start/stop RPC listeners (FNDFS/FNDSM)
- adcmctl.sh start/stop Concurrent Manager

- gsmstart.sh — start/stop FNDSM
- jtffmctl.sh — start/stop Fulfillment Server
- adpreclone.pl — cloning preparation script
- adoafmctl.sh — start/stop/status OC4J oafm (webservice, mapviewer)
- adexecsql.pl — Execute sql scripts that update the profiles in an AutoConfig run
- java.sh — It calls java executable with additional args, (used by opmn, Conc. Mgr)

29. Explain briefly the various environment variable changes in 11i and R12.

The environment variable changes between 11i and R12 is given in the table below.

ENVIRONMENT FILES/VARIABLE CHANGES

	Old	New
Env Source File	APPSORA.env	APPS<SID>.env This file executes the following env files $ORA_CONFIG_HOME/ 10.1.2/$TWO_TASK.env $APPL_CONFIG_HOME/ $TWO_TASK.env
Context File (MT)	$APPL_TOP/admin/ $TWO_TASK.xml	$APPL_CONFIG_ HOME/admin/ $TWO_TASK.xml
OA_HTML	$COMMON_TOP/ html	$COMMON_TOP/ webapps/oacore/html
JAVA_TOP, OA_ JAVA	$COMMON_TOP/ java	$COMMON_TOP/java/ classes
AF_JLIB	N/A	$COMMON_TOP/java/lib
JAVA_BASE	N/A	$COMMON_TOP/java/

(*Contd*)

	Old	**New**
FND_SECURE	$FND_TOP/secure/<SID>/	$INST_TOP/apps/fnd/12.0.0/secure/
ADMIN_SCRIPTS_HOME	$COMMON_TOP/admin/scripts/<SID>/	$INST_TOP/admin/scripts/
LOG_HOME	$APPL_TOP/admin/<SID>/logs/	$INST_TOP/logs
FORMS_WEB_CONFIG_FILE	N/A	$INST_TOP/ora/10.1.2/forms/server/appsweb.cfg

30. What is the concept of unified APPL_TOP in R12?

R12 introduces the concept of unified APPL_TOP which means everything is laid down on all servers. From the APPL_TOP perspective, all the servers on a multi-node environment will have the same files and can now potentially start any service if needed. In some cases, additional configuration will be required before this can be done since there can be profiles, etc. associated with each server.

For R12, the only difference between the servers, are the services that have been activated on each node.

The services are identified by the variables on the / service_group/ section in the Apps Context File:

* Root Service Group: s_root_status

* Web Entry Point Services: s_web_entry_status

* Web Application Services: s_web_applications_status

* Batch Processing Services: s_batch_status

* Other Service Group: s_other_service_group_status

Depending on the value of these variables (enabled or disabled), adstrtal.sh/adstpall.sh will only start/stop the services associated with them, ignoring the rest.

31. How is Oracle Application Server 10g integrated with Oracle E-Business Suite R12?

The Oracle E-Business Suite R12 uses several individual components delivered as part of the Oracle Application Server suite. These individual components include the Oracle HTTP Server (powered by Apache), PL/SQL, Forms Server, Reports Server, Workflow and many others.

In particular, E-Business Suite R12 uses OracleAS 10g 10.1.2 for Forms and Reports Services, replacing the 8.0.6-based ORACLE_HOME provided by the Oracle9i Application Server 1.0.2.2.2 in E-Business Suite Release 11i. In addition, E-Business Suite R12 uses OracleAS 10g 10.1.3 for Oracle containers for J2EE (OC4J), replacing the 8.1.7-based ORACLE_HOME provided by Oracle9i Application Server 1.0.2.2.2 in E-Business Suite Release 11i.

32. How can you edit the CONTEXT_FILE?

You can edit the CONTEXT_FILE from Oracle Applications Manager by clicking the site map and then by clicking the edit parameter button. Directly changing the xml file is not recommended as there are many dependencis among the parameters which the OAM takes care.

33. You have accidentally deleted the CONTEXT_FILE. How will you recreate the same?

You can recreate the control file using the script "adclonectx.pl retrieve" located at COMMON_TOP>/clone/bin. In R12 the adbldxml.pl can no longer be used.

34. How can I determine whether an autoconfig template is customizable or non-customizable?

If a keyword "LOCK" is present at the end of the file entry in the respective driver, it is a non-customizable template. If the "LOCK" keyword is not seen, that template can be customized.

35. In R12, the default mode for the forms is servlet mode. How can you change from servlet to socket mode?

You need to run the script "txkrun.pl" located at $FND_TOP to toggle between the socket and servlet mode. You are also required to run autoconfig.

36. What are the patching enhancements in R12?

The following are the enhancements in patching in R12.

- The patching in R12 introduces Manual Steps Infrastructure (MSI) functionality, reducing the number and complexity of manual steps.
- The patch wizard is now more enhanced for identifying, downloading and analyzing recommended patches.
- The risk of patch breaking other functionality is reduced in R12 as now it supports for checking codelevels and baselines.
- You can have patch filters in R12 to search patches specific to your environment.

37. What is Support Identifier (CSI) number?

It is the unique Customer Support Identifier number provided by Oracle. It is used to open Service Request against Oracle for any issues coming in the Application system.

38. What is the fastest way to create an application system in R12?

Express Configuration is the fastest way to create an application system in R12. It can configure a single node/single user system with either a fresh database or Vision Demo database.

39. What can I do if I am unable to find solution to a question?

If you are stuck in any tricky question and unable to find a solution, feel free to write to me at joyjeet.books@gmail.com.

Index

<sid>.xml 19
8.0.6 22
8.0.6 Oracle Home 4
9iAS 16

A

access_log 6
access_log_pls 6
ActiveX 2
Ad splice 83
Ad utilities 19, 76
Adadmin 77
Adaimgr 104
adapcctl.sh 6, 22
adapcctl.txt 22
adautostg.pl 26
adcfgclone.pl 98
Adclone 90
adconfig.txt 17
adfrmctl.sh 22
adgebdbc.sh 10
adjareas.txt 17
adjborg.txt 17
adjborg2.txt 17
Admin server 1, 5, 11
AdminAppServer 10
adovars.env 19
Adpatch 63
adpltfrm.txt 17
Adrelink 88
adrepctl.sh 23
Adrepgen 15
adstpall.sh 23
adstrtal.sh 23
adutconf.sql 31
AOL diagnostics 9, 10
Apache 5, 9, 11
Apache configuration 6
Apache log 6
Apachectl 6
APPL_TOP 17
APPLET 13
Application tier 4
Applmgr 25
APPLSYSPUB 19
Apps password 21
apps.conf 6, 7
APPSORA.env 17
appsweb.cfg 15, 17

Architecture 1
Autoconfig 7

B

Bis 16
Business intelligence 15
Business Intelligence System 16

C

C driver 62
Cache 71
CGI 12
Client desktop 2
Client tier 4
Cloning 90
cmclean.sql 48
COMMON_TOP 119
CONCSUB 45
Concurrent manager 11, 42
Concurrent processing server 1, 5, 11, 15
Concurrent program 58
Concurrent requests 11
config.txt 28
Configuration files 17, 27
Conflict resolution manager 43
CONSCUB 50
CONTEXT_FILE 21, 128
CONTEXT_NAME 16

D

D driver 62
Database tier 3
DBC 10
DBC file 18
Debug 9
Defaults file 65
Desktop clients 12
Direct forms 40
Directories 26
Discoverer 16
Discoverer 4i 16
Discoverer server 1, 5, 16
Disk requirement 24
Disks 25
Distributed AD? 85
DomainName 18
DUAL table 83

E

ec 16
E-commerce 16
error_log 6
error_log_pls 6
Express configuration 27

F

f60ctl 22
f60svrm.txt 22
f60webmx 14, 22, 37
FMB file 37
FND 20
FND_CONCURRENT_REQUESTS 52
FND_INSTALL_PROCESSES 73
FND_NODES 21
FND_ORACLE_USERID 20
FND_TOP 7, 17
FND_USERS 20
FNDCPASS 20

FNDLIBR 49
FNDLOAD 20
FNDNAM 18
FNDSVCRG 23
Forms client applet 2
Forms Listener 13
Forms Runtime Diagnostics 36
Forms runtime engine 14
Forms server 1, 4, 12, 22, 36
Forms Server Name 18
Forms users 14
FORMS60_CATCHTERM 39
FORMS60_TIMEOUT 37
FRD 36
Fresh install 24

G

G driver 63
Generate message files 81
GWYUID 18

H

Hostname_SID.dbc 17
HTML 6
HTTP Listener 12, 13
httpd.conf 6, 8, 9
httpds.conf 9

I

IAS_CONFIG_HOME 7
IAS_ORACLE_HOME 8, 11
ICX: forms launcher 39
Instance Top 116
Internal concurrent manager 42
Internal manager 42
Internal monitor 48
Internet Explorer 2

J

JAR 2, 13
Java Applet 13
Java Archive 2, 13
Java Server Pages 5
Java Servlet Engine 5
Java Virtual Machine 2
JDBC 10
JDBC thin client 19
JDBC URL 10
JInitator 2, 13
Jserv 5, 8, 9
jserv.conf 8, 9
jserv.properties 7, 8, 9
JVM 13

L

Load balancing 12, 14, 30
LogLevel 9

M

Maintenance mode 76
Maintenance pack 61
Middle tier 15
Minipack 61
MMB file 37
mod_jserv.log. 8
mod_pls 11
modplsql 22
multi-node 21

Multi-node cloning 93
Multi-node installation 28, 29, 68
Multiple node installation 93

N

Netscape Navigator 2
NLS 26

O

OA_HTML 18
OATM 21
OC4J 113
ODF 89
ojsp.conf 8
OPMN 114
OPMN.XML 120
oraAppDB 26
oraApps 26
Oracle Applications 1
Oracle e-business suite 16
Oracle Home 4
Oracle HTTP server 5
oracle_apache.conf 8
ORACLE_HOME 16
OracleAS 10g 128
oraDB 26
oraiAS 26
oraNLS 26
ORION-APPLICATION.XML 120
ORION-WEB.XML 120

P

Parallel concurrent processing 53, 54
Patch 61, 63
Patch history 100
PL/SQL logging 11
PLL file 37
plsql cache 10
PMON 53
Post-upgrade 110
Pre-install checks 26, 32
Pre-upgrade 101
Process 11
Product 16
Production database 24
PUB 19

R

RAC 10
Rapidclone 90, 91
RapidInstall 24, 25, 26
RapidInstall log 33
RapidInstall Wizard 27
Real application clusters 4
Release 12 112
Reports server 1, 4, 15, 23, 119
Request id 20
Restart files 69
rwmts60 15

S

Scripts 125
SERVER.XML 120
Service groups 123, 124
Servlet engine 5
Servlet mode 41
shared APPL_TOP 7, 29, 93
Shared application tier file system 29

SID 10
SID.xml 17
Single node 24
Single node installation 27, 93
Snapshot 86
Socket 13
Socket mode 41
Stage area 24
Standard manager 43
StartCD 26
SUPPORT_ADMIN 21
SUPPORT_CP 21
SUPPORT_DB 21
SUPPORT_FORMS 21
SUPPPORT_WEB 21

T

Tablespace 21
TCF 22
TCP/IP 13
Technology stack 4
Test mode 66
Thin client 14
Tier 1
Topfile.txt 17
Trace 57
Tracing 40
TUMS 101
TWO_TASK 18

U

U driver 63
unified APPL_TOP 127

V

Validate APPS schema 82
View 75
Vision Demo database 24, 27

W

Web listener 5
Web server 1
Windows 2
Work shift 59

Z

zone.properties 8

2695248

Made in the USA